The Book of Jeremiah

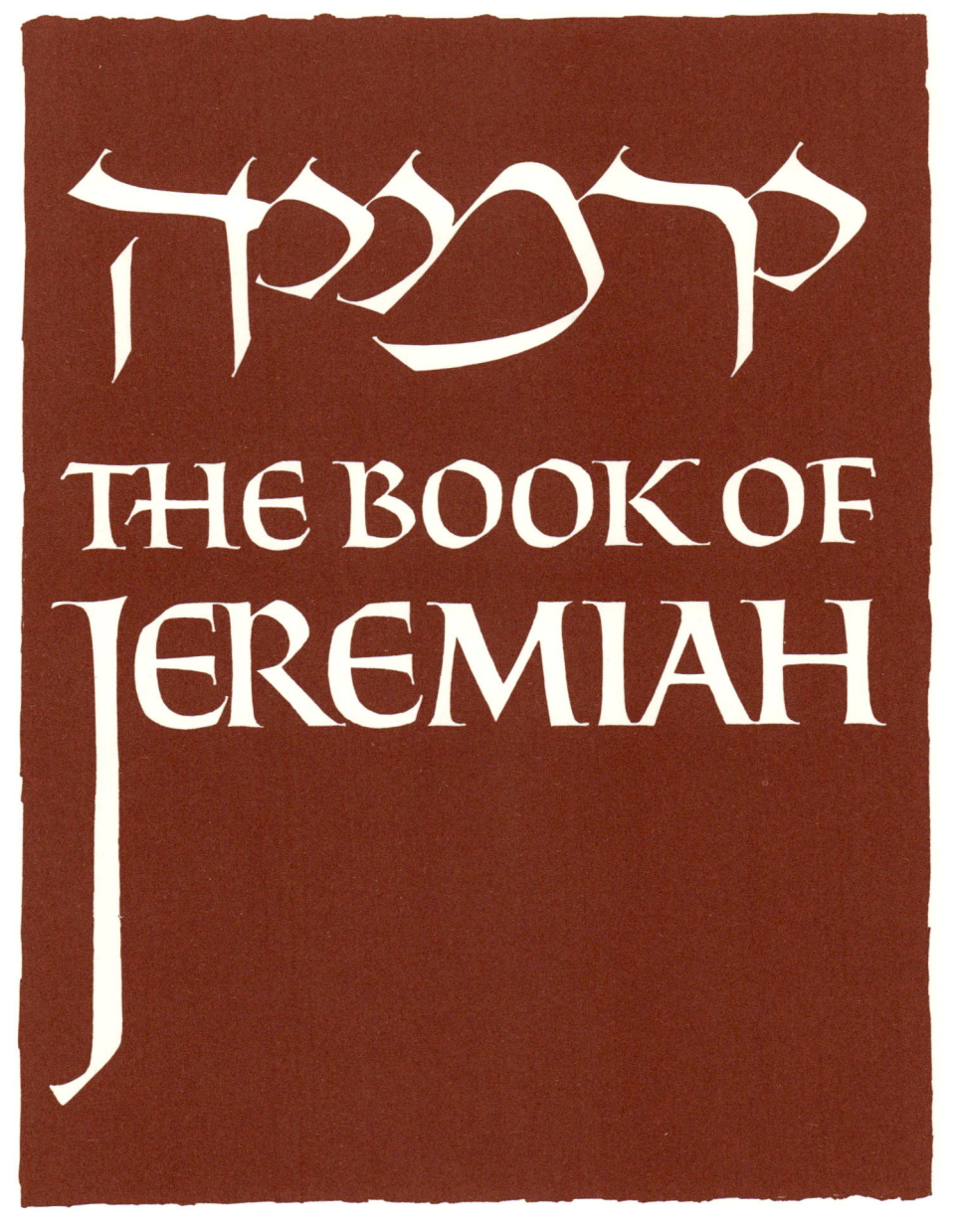

ירמיה
THE BOOK OF JEREMIAH

A NEW TRANSLATION

WITH WOODCUTS BY *Nikos Stavroulakis*

INTRODUCTION BY *Bernard J. Bamberger*

The Jewish Publication Society of America, Philadelphia

COPYRIGHT © 1973 BY THE JEWISH PUBLICATION SOCIETY OF AMERICA
FIRST EDITION • ALL RIGHTS RESERVED
ISBN 0-8276-0027-5
LIBRARY OF CONGRESS CATALOG CARD NUMBER 73–3911
MANUFACTURED IN THE UNITED STATES OF AMERICA
DESIGNED BY ISMAR DAVID

COMMITTEE OF TRANSLATORS OF THE NEVIIM
Editor-in-chief H. L. GINSBERG • *Fellow Editor* HARRY M. ORLINSKY
Associate Editors MAX ARZT, BERNARD J. BAMBERGER, HARRY FRIEDMAN,
SOLOMON GRAYZEL, *Secretary*

INTRODUCTION

Bernard J. Bamberger

JEREMIAH AND THE MODERN READER

To the popular mind the name Jeremiah suggests the picture of an old man crushed by incurable grief. This is doubtless due to the old tradition that Jeremiah wrote the Book of Lamentations, that outpouring of sorrow over the fall of Jerusalem. (Only once does it venture as far as a cautious "there may yet be hope," Lamentations 3.29.) But modern scholars, with good reason, deny that Jeremiah wrote Lamentations: the elegies of which it consists, though deeply felt, are conventional in form and style, and in substance they sometimes disagree with Jeremiah's thinking.

It is true that Jeremiah predicted the downfall of the nation; and he never stopped grieving over the course of events, and over his own obligation to speak distasteful truths. None of the prophets who lived before the Exile was a jolly, "well-adjusted" personality. But these men were not mere harbingers of doom. They were the spokesmen of powerful ethical imperatives, rooted in profound religious experience. Some of them, at least, had a vision of national rebirth and renewal that would follow the approaching catastrophe. Jeremiah especially was a prophet of hope. At the very moment of his call to prophecy, he was given a mission not only "To uproot and to pull down, / To destroy and to overthrow," but also "To build and to plant" (1.10). The same man who warned a complacent generation of disaster to come spoke of redemption and future glory when the disaster was at hand and those who had been so smug were in a state of panic and despair.

On first reading, Jeremiah seems to speak in predominantly negative terms: he castigates and threatens. The reason is that he was speaking directly to the circumstances of his own time, and therefore attacked concrete and specific injustices. But out of his negations a positive and vivid concept of justice emerges. Though he did not consciously write for posterity, Jeremiah delivered a message of enduring worth.

Throughout history, Israel's prophets have been an inspiration to those who sought to build a more fair and compassionate society. "Jeremiah," says a modern commentator, "is companion to the daring" (Sheldon H. Blank, *Jeremiah: Man and Prophet*, p. 231). He has much to say to us, in a time when men are torn between a foolish optimism and an unrelieved hopelessness. An inspiring personality and a gifted poet, he sets before us the perennial issue of values:

> Let not the wise man glory in his wisdom;
> Let not the strong man glory in his strength;
> Let not the rich man glory in his riches.
> But only in this should one glory:
> In his earnest devotion to Me.
> For I the LORD act with kindness,
> Justice, and equity in the world;
> For in these I delight
>
> —declares the LORD. (9.22–23)

Jeremiah is of special importance for another reason: through him we gain a much better understanding of all biblical prophecy.

For the prophets of Israel —above all, those designated as *neviim aḥaronim*, "later prophets"—constitute a unique phenomenon in human history. The ancient Near Eastern literatures that have been brought to light in the past century contain numerous resemblances, occasionally even verbal parallels, to the narratives, laws, poetry, and wisdom books of the Hebrew Bible. (It goes without saying that these resemblances should not be overstressed. The originality of the Bible has not been put into question by these discoveries.) But there is nothing in the old Near Eastern sources, or in any other literature, that really resembles the utterances of the Hebrew prophets.

All peoples have had their seers, fortune tellers, diviners, augurs. The prophets of Israel were men of another sort. "A prophet," says Professor Blank, "deserves honor not because he foresees the coming event, but because he sees the meaning within the current event. It is the prophet's gift of insight, not his foresight, that sets him apart" (ibid., p. 4). The prophets regarded themselves as literally the spokesmen of God, bringing to king and commoner the message He had charged them with. They seem not to have been disturbed if their predictions were not fulfilled to the letter; they did not feel the need to "correct" such statements. Their basic task was to declare God's will, not to forecast events. (In addition to these men, Israel had official, professional *neviim*, whom such men as Jeremiah denounced as "false prophets." But we should not assume that they were all corrupt time-servers. In all generations, many adherents of the "establishment" have believed sincerely in establishment policies and institutions, and have regarded dissenters and critics as a menace to public welfare. See Jeremiah 23.9 ff., and chapters 27 and 28.)

The prophetic movement lasted for three centuries or more. A substantial number of the prophetic messages has been preserved, comprising 232 chapters. Yet we know very little about the men who produced them. The biographical details that appear occasionally are as a rule brief and tantalizing. About some prophets we know nothing but their names; for others, notably the unknown who wrote chapters 40–66 of Isaiah, we do not even have a name.

Jeremiah is the important exception. His book contains many narrative chapters, dealing with critical events in his long career. Even more precious are a number of moving passages in which Jeremiah opens his heart and talks with his God. These so-called confessions, written down by Jeremiah for no one's use but his own and preserved, it well may be, by accident, give us an extraordinary insight into the prophet's thoughts and feelings as he struggles with frustration, crisis, and tragedy. (The most important passages, in addition to Jeremiah's call to prophecy, chapter 1, are 11.18–23; 12.1–6; 15.15–21; 17.14–18, and perhaps others: parts of chapters 16 and 17; 18.18–23; 20.7–13; and 20.14–18.)

THE LIFE OF JEREMIAH

Jeremiah came from a priestly family located at Anathoth, not far from Jerusalem. He spent most of his life in the capital, but there is no record that he ever officiated as a priest.

He was probably born early in the reign of Josiah (641/640 – 609 B.C.E.). This king came to the throne as a child. In his formative years he was greatly influenced by the religious teachers of his time. After he assumed the duties of government, he undertook a far-reaching religious reformation (II Kings 22 and 23); he outlawed the foreign cults which had flourished in Judah during the reigns of his father and grandfather. In addition, he abolished all the local shrines scattered throughout the country, which, though dedicated to the God of Israel, may have preserved some vestiges of

Canaanite practice. Henceforth sacrifice was permitted only at the Temple in Jerusalem, where supervision by the king and the official priesthood was to keep worship pure of any pagan admixture. These reforms, based on Deuteronomy 12, were completed about 622/621 B.C.E.

Jeremiah does not refer explicitly to this reformation and does not seem to have been involved in it. In one passage he declares that the alleged piety of Judah was no more than pretense, and that it was more offensive to God than the out-and-out idolatry of the Northern Kingdom had been (3.6 ff.). This passage may reflect disillusionment with Josiah's reforms. For idolatry had not been eradicated, but only driven underground; a few years later the people were again openly practicing pagan rites (7.17 ff.; cf. chapter 44).

But Jeremiah's primary concern was not with cult. Like all his great predecessors, he taught that God must be served by the practice of justice and righteousness in personal and in national life. Now, it is unlikely that the moral life of Judah was inferior to that of other nations, but that did not satisfy the prophets. Exploitation, corruption, cruelty, treachery did exist; theft, murder, adultery did occur. Measured by the exacting standard of God's law, Judah had to be adjudged faithless.

And so, from the beginning of his ministry, Jeremiah announced the impending downfall of the nation—unless there should be a radical change of heart, manifest in deeds of goodness and humanity, and in the rejection of all forms of idolatry.

In his earlier prophecies, Jeremiah declared that the divine punishment would be inflicted by peoples of the kingdoms of the north (1.15, 6.22), who would invade the land, devastate it, and pillage it. Jeremiah does not state specifically who the northern invaders would be, and scholars have debated the question as to what people or peoples he had in mind. To me it seems at least possible that he was referring to the great military empire of Assyria, which had dominated western Asia for centuries. (Armies from Mesopotamia invariably entered Palestine from the north.) This great power, however, was in decline; it was virtually destroyed in 612 B.C.E. by a coalition of Medes and Chaldeans. In the ensuing decade, the Chaldean (or neo-Babylonian) Empire imposed its rule upon the entire Near East. But for a time Egypt resisted this expansion. Pharaoh Necho moved northward through Palestine to establish a base on the Euphrates. King Josiah tried to stop him at Megiddo, and his courageous act led to complete disaster. Josiah was killed, and Judah was reduced to vassalage.

Josiah's son Shallum (or Jehoahaz), who had succeeded his father, was deposed by the Egyptians and deported; he was replaced by his brother Eliakim, who was given the regnal name of Jehoiakim.

The new king willingly collaborated with Egypt; when, some years later, the Chaldeans drove back the Egyptians and imposed their control upon Judah, Jehoiakim submitted and was allowed to retain his throne.

The defeat and death of Josiah posed grave religious problems. The Torah declared, and the prophets had taught, that loyalty to Israel's God would be rewarded with prosperity and long life; yet Josiah, so outstanding in his fidelity, had been destroyed. The religious leaders could find no solution to the problem and took refuge in silence. Jeremiah speaks of the dead king with great admiration (22.15–16), but does not explain his tragic end. (See Stanley Brice Frost, "The Death of Josiah: A Conspiracy of Silence," *Journal of Biblical Literature*, December 1968, pp. 369 ff.) But some of the people inferred from the disaster that Josiah's reforms were not acceptable; they held that recognition ought to be given to other powers besides the God of the Jerusalem Temple (see 44.17–18).

Jehoiakim was in no way his father's son. Josiah had resisted the Egyptians, Jehoiakim was their docile follower. But what infuriated Jeremiah was the king's indifference to the rights and the welfare of his people, while he indulged himself in lavish expenditures for pretentious and luxurious living (22.13–19).

With such an example of irresponsibility at the top, moral corruption was bound to spread through the people. And so, on a festive occasion when throngs from all over Judah were gathered at the Temple, Jeremiah appeared and vehemently denounced their worship as obnoxious to God, because it was not accompanied by ethical living. The Temple, which they believed to be inviolable, would not protect them; they had made it into a den of robbers, and God would destroy it as He had once destroyed the sanctuary at Shiloh (7.1—8.23).

Jeremiah's words outraged his hearers; his prediction that the Temple would be destroyed appeared to them as treason and sacrilege. He barely escaped with his life (chapter 26).

Several years later, on another public festival, Jeremiah's prophecies were read to the people by his follower and amanuensis, Baruch son of Neriah. Again the blunt words of threat and denunciation created an uproar. Some of the royal councilors questioned Baruch; after hearing the contents of his scroll, they advised him to go into hiding and to keep Jeremiah out of sight. And they confiscated the scroll, which the king later cut up and burned with his own hands. Jeremiah thereupon dictated again the entire contents of the scroll, and added more prophecies to it (chapter 36). Apparently the prophet and his follower remained "underground" during most of Jehoiakim's reign.

We have seen that this king was allowed to keep his throne when control of Palestine was taken by the Chaldeans under their powerful king, Nebuchadrezzar. (This is the usual spelling of the name in the Book of Jeremiah; it is closer to the Babylonian original than the more familiar form, Nebuchadnezzar.) But Jehoiakim and many of his courtiers were pro-Egyptian at heart; they again became involved in intrigue with Egyptian agents. In 598 B.C.E. they took the first steps of revolt against the Chaldean overlord. Nebuchadrezzar's forces moved promptly against Jerusalem, which surrendered after a short siege (597 B.C.E.). By that time Jehoiakim had died or been assassinated and had been succeeded by his son Jehoiachin (the Coniah of Jeremiah 22.24 ff.). The latter was carried off to Babylon as a prisoner; another son of Josiah, Zedekiah, took an oath of fealty to the Chaldean ruler, and was installed on the throne. He was apparently a well-intentioned man and was favorably disposed to Jeremiah; but he lacked strength of will and found it hard to resist the pro-Egyptian pressures which the court began to exert on him.

During the reign of Zedekiah, Jeremiah was once more active in public. His addresses were sometimes underscored by symbolic actions (chapters 18, 19, 27, 28)—a procedure followed by other prophets as well. But his hearers found his message as unpalatable as ever. It could not have been otherwise. He made slashing attacks on corrupt officialdom; he castigated the people for their immorality and pagan practices; and he denounced as liars the popular prophets who were predicting the speedy downfall of the Chaldeans and the return of the exiles.

For Jeremiah had come to more definite opinions about the course of history. Formerly, as we saw, he had envisioned the punishment of Judah as an invasion by unspecified peoples from the north, who would pillage and devastate the land. Now he was convinced that the penalty was to be not merely destruction but subjugation. Nebuchadrezzar was God's chosen agent in history—for the time being. Resistance to the Chaldeans would not only be futile—it would be disobedience to God. Submission would ward off greater disaster. And when in good time the Babylonian power had fulfilled its mission, it would come to an end and Judah would be restored.

Along with Coniah, a considerable number of persons had been deported to Babylonia: members of the nobility, military, and priesthood, as well as skilled craftsmen—the kind of people who might be key figures in a rebellion. Jeremiah was in correspondence with these exiles; he urged them to sink roots into their new land, where they would have to remain for a long time. Only after seventy years (a conventional round number meaning "a considerable time," as in Isaiah 23.15) would Judah be redeemed (chapter 29). Jeremiah had great hopes for this community, which he believed was more decent and pious than those who remained in the homeland (chapter 24). Incidentally, this first Jewish diaspora, in Babylonia, continued to exist without interruption for some 2,400 years, until the recent liquidation of the Jewish community of Iraq.

Jeremiah's "pro-Babylonian" attitude made him an easy target for those who resented his searching criticism. He was a treasonous agent of the Chaldeans, they declared, seeking to undermine national morale. And so he was constantly the object of hatred and hostility. On at least one occasion he was arrested and flogged (chapter 20); he was constantly slandered and abused. It was probably in these years that many of the "confessions" were composed. In these infinitely touching fragments he pours out his grief, complains of persecution, and occasionally invokes punishment on his tormentors. He voices his own faith, and he records the divine responses he received—responses which were challenging rather than soothing.

In one of the most striking of these passages he presents the prophetic dilemma. The prophets of Israel were not contemplative mystics who cultivated a vision of the divine. The call of God came to them unsought; Jeremiah, like Moses, tried to evade the summons (1.6 ff.; cf. Exodus 3.11—4.13). When Jeremiah discovered that the consequences of speaking the divine word were scorn, hatred, and injury, he tried to keep silent. But the undelivered message could not be suppressed (20.7–13); it

> ... was like a raging fire in my heart,
> Shut up in my bones;
> I could not hold it in, I was helpless.

The confessions of Jeremiah are among the earliest documents of what we call today "personal religion."

Eventually the pro-Egyptian forces at the court could no longer be resisted. Zedekiah withheld tribute from the Chaldeans, and the rebellion was under way. The struggle was hopeless from the start; but for a time, when the pace of Nebuchadrezzar's punitive expedition was slowed by the approach of Egyptian armies and other distractions, the rebels were encouraged. Jeremiah urged them to submit to the Chaldeans; for this he was called traitor and confined in a military compound. On at least one occasion his enemies tried to do away with him; but an Ethiopian slave notified the king, and Jeremiah was rescued (chapter 38). The Chaldean armies surrounded Jerusalem. This time the siege lasted a year and a half, until sheer hunger prevented the defenders from fighting effectively. The city fell and the Temple was burned in the summer of 587 B.C.E.

As the end was approaching and the certainty of doom was plain to all, Jeremiah gave dramatic expression to his own deep faith. He acquired title to some family property while it was occupied by Chaldean troops; by the publicity he gave the transaction, and by his careful arrangements to preserve the deed, he made vivid his expectation that Judah would ultimately be restored through God's grace (32.6 ff.). Perhaps, too, it is in this period that we should date his teaching concerning the new covenant which God will write, not on tablets of stone like the covenant of Sinai, but on the very hearts of the regenerated people (31.31 ff.).

After the fall of Jerusalem, large numbers of the people were deported. The government of those who remained was entrusted by the Chaldeans to a certain Gedaliah. Jeremiah was offered the opportunity to go to Babylon as a "guest" of the conquerors, but chose to remain in the land of Israel.

Before Gedaliah could begin the work of reconstruction, he was murdered by a member of the royal family, who apparently hoped to start a new revolt against Babylon. The rebellion was never launched; but the few remaining leaders in Judah were completely shaken by Gedaliah's death. Fearing that they would be held responsible by the Chaldeans for what had happened, they proposed flight to Egypt. But first they came to Jeremiah for prophetic guidance. He urged them to remain in the land, declaring that this was God's will, and that it would be to their benefit. Evidently that was not what they wanted to hear. Jeremiah, they asserted, was the dupe of his disciple Baruch, who wanted to betray them to the Chaldeans. They insisted on going to Egypt, and forced Jeremiah to accompany them. Our last glimpses of the aged prophet are on Egyptian soil. With seemingly undiminished vigor, he is warning the people against the pagan observances he had so often condemned in

Jerusalem, and which they continued or revived after they arrived in Egypt (chapters 40–44).

Thus throughout his life Jeremiah was outwardly defeated and frustrated. But he never gave up his trust in the God who rules history, and who he was sure would right accumulated wrongs and restore the remnant of His people to their land, purified from injustice and idolatry.

THE BOOK OF JEREMIAH

Even a superficial examination reveals that the Book of Jeremiah is made up of two kinds of writing. Large sections are poetry which, like all good poetry, has a distinctive tone and flavor. Though much of it consists of warnings of the coming doom, it is lyrical rather than declamatory. Jeremiah's poetry reminds us of the tender pleadings of Hosea rather than the thunder of Amos. As he announces the impending destruction, he himself mourns over the evil tidings he must transmit.

Other sections of the book are in vigorous but somewhat stereotyped prose, similar in style to the rhetoric of Deuteronomy. These prose sections are largely narrative, but also include prophecies ascribed to Jeremiah.

Because the two kinds of writing in the book are so markedly different, a Christian scholar named Duhm argued in 1901 that only the poetic sections are genuine prophecies of Jeremiah, and the rest of the book is late and inauthentic. This radical view has rightly been rejected by most modern commentators. In substance and spirit, there is nothing more Jeremian than such prose passages as the Temple sermon (7.1—8.3) and the denunciation of those who first liberated their Hebrew slaves and then forced them back into slavery (34.8 ff.). The bulk of the book, both poetry and prose, is a reliable source for the prophet's life and teaching. (It is noteworthy that the narratives contain no miraculous or other legendary elements.) In all probability, the book is based on the compilation made by Baruch. The poetic oracles were written down from the prophet's dictation; in the prose sections, Baruch recorded events as he witnessed them or heard about them; and he reproduced the substance, though not the exact wording, of what the prophet said. We cannot prove this thesis, but it is a plausible explanation of the data.

This does not preclude the possibility (in this writer's opinion it is a certainty) that the present Book of Jeremiah contains a number of insertions and additions. Thus we have two accounts (37.16–21 and 38.14–28) of a secret interview between King Zedekiah and the prophet. It seems unlikely that there were two such meetings; more probably, we have two versions of the same incident. The latter part of chapter 32, though substantially authentic, seems somewhat padded, as if a copyist tried to "improve" the style by adding phrases and clauses. There are many other such instances.

One extensive portion which appears to me to be predominantly, if not entirely, non-Jeremian is the series of oracles against foreign nations in chapters 46 through 51. They predict disaster for the enemies of Judah; in a few cases they gloat over disaster that has already occurred. They display little or nothing of the ethical and religious concerns of Jeremiah; in spirit and style they are much like the oracles against the nations found in other prophetic books. And they contain some of the same material. The oracle on Moab (chapter 48) draws upon the document in Isaiah 15 and 16 (which may well be older than Isaiah's time) and cites Isaiah 24.17–18 almost word for word. The prophecy against Edom (49.7 ff.) contains material also found in Obadiah. At least some parts of the oracle against Babylon (chapters 50 and 51) appear to have been composed after the fall of that city, when Jeremiah had been dead for decades.

The narrative passages in Jeremiah 39 and 52 reproduce II Kings 25, with variants and additions.

The reader will also note that various chapters, and sometimes parts of chapters, are not in order; passages that date from different times are joined, and vice versa. Chapter 22 is an extreme instance: verses 10–12 refer to Shallum (also called Jehoahaz, II Kings 23.31 ff.), who was deposed by Pharaoh Necho in 609 B.C.E. Verses 13–19 are an attack on his successor, Jehoiakim, and must date from a few years later. And verses 24–30 lament the deportation of Jehoiakim's son Coniah (or Jehoiachin, II Kings 24.8 ff.) to Babylon in 597 B.C.E.!

Chapter 26 deals with the Temple sermon of 7.1—8.3, and the consequences of its delivery, early in the reign of Jehoiakim. Chapters 35 and 36 are likewise dated explicitly in Jehoiakim's reign, though they are preceded and followed by reports of events in the kingship of Zedekiah. Also dated in the reign of Jehoiakim is the brief address to Baruch, chapter 45. (Composed when the two men were probably fugitives, it is strangely lacking in personal warmth.) Yet this chapter follows the long narrative in 39–44 of events following the fall of Jerusalem and of Jeremiah's exile in Egypt.

(It should be noted also that the old Greek translation [the Septuagint] of Jeremiah departs widely from the Hebrew text in many places. In particular, the oracles against the foreign nations, which in the Hebrew text are grouped near the end of the book [chapters 46–51] are located in the Greek after 25.13.)

Despite these elements of confusion, the reader will find the Book of Jeremiah easier to understand and appreciate than most of the other prophetic writings. And in the long run, his acquaintance with the prophet will prove to be not a depressing, but an uplifting experience.

THE BOOK OF JEREMIAH

1

¹ The words of Jeremiah son of Hilkiah, one of the priests at Anathoth in the territory of Benjamin. ² The word of the LORD came to him in the days of King Josiah son of Amon of Judah, in the thirteenth year of his reign, ³ and throughout the days of King Jehoiakim son of Josiah of Judah, and until the end of the eleventh year of King Zedekiah son of Josiah of Judah, when Jerusalem went into exile in the fifth month.

JEREMIAH 1·4

⁴ The word of the LORD came to me:

⁵ Before I created you in the womb, I selected you;
Before you were born, I consecrated you;
I appointed you a prophet concerning the nations.

⁶ I replied:

Ah, Lord GOD!
I don't know how to speak,
For I am still a boy.
⁷ And the LORD said to me:

Do not say, I am still a boy,
But go wherever I send you
And speak whatever I command you.
⁸ Have no fear of them,
For I am with you to deliver you
—declares the LORD.

⁹ The LORD put out His hand and touched my mouth, and the LORD said to me: Herewith I put My words into your mouth.
¹⁰ See, I appoint you this day
Over nations and kingdoms:
To uproot and to pull down,
To destroy and to overthrow,
To build and to plant.

¹¹ The word of the LORD came to me: What do you see, Jeremiah? I replied: I see a branch of an almond tree.ᵃ

¹² The LORD said to me:
You have seen right,
For I am watchfulᵇ to bring My word to pass.
¹³ And the word of the LORD came to me a second time: What do you see? I replied:
I see a steaming pot,
ᶜ⁻Tipped away from the north.⁻ᶜ
¹⁴ And the LORD said to me:
From the north shall disaster break loose
Upon all the inhabitants of the land!
¹⁵ For I am summoning all the peoples
of the kingdoms of the north
—declares the LORD.
They shall come, and shall each set up a throne
Before the gates of Jerusalem,
Against its walls round about
And against all the towns of Judah.

ᵃHeb *shaqed*
ᵇHeb *shoqed*
ᶜ⁻ᶜMeaning of Heb uncertain

16 And I will argue My case against them[d]
 For all their wickedness:
 They have forsaken Me
 And sacrificed to other gods
 And worshiped the works of their hands.

17 So you, gird up your loins,
 Arise and speak to them
 All that I command you.
 Do not break down before them,
 Lest I break you before them.
18 I make you this day
 A fortified city,
 And an iron pillar,
 And bronze walls
 Against the whole land—
 Against Judah's kings and officers,
 And against its priests and citizens.[e]
19 They will attack you,
 But they shall not overcome you;
 For I am with you—declares the LORD—to save you.

2

¹ The word of the LORD came to me, saying, ² Go proclaim to Jerusalem: Thus said the LORD:
 I accounted to your favor
 The devotion of your youth,
 Your love as a bride—
 How you followed Me in the wilderness,
 In a land not sown.
³ Israel was holy to the LORD,
 The first fruits of His harvest.
 All who ate of it were held guilty;
 Disaster befell them
 —declares the LORD.

⁴ Hear the word of the LORD, O House of Jacob,
 Every clan of the House of Israel!
⁵ Thus said the LORD:

 What wrong did your fathers find in Me
 That they abandoned Me
 And went after delusion and deluded themselves?
⁶ They never asked themselves, "Where is the LORD,
 Who brought us up from the land of Egypt,
 Who led us through the wilderness,
 A land of deserts and pits,
 A land of drought and darkness,
 A land no man had traversed,
 Where no human being had dwelt?"
⁷ I brought you to this country of farmland
 To enjoy its fruit and its bounty.
 But you came and defiled My land,
 You made My possession abhorrent.
⁸ The priests never asked themselves, "Where is the LORD?"
 The guardians of the Teaching ignored Me;
 The rulers[a] rebelled against Me,
 And the prophets prophesied by Baal
 And followed what can do no good.
⁹ Oh, I will go on accusing you
 —declares the LORD—
 And I will accuse your children's children!
¹⁰ Just cross over to the isles of the Kittim and look,
 Send to Kedar and observe carefully;
 See if aught like this has ever happened:
¹¹ Has any nation changed its gods
 Even though they are no-gods?
 But My people has exchanged its glory
 For what can do no good.
¹² Be appalled, O heavens, at this;
 Be horrified, utterly dazed!
 —declares the LORD.
¹³ For My people have done a twofold wrong:
 They forsook Me, the Fount of living waters,
 And hewed them out cisterns, broken cisterns,
 Which cannot even hold water.

¹⁴ Is Israel a bondman?
 Is he a home-born slave?
 Then why is he given over to plunder?
¹⁵ Lions have roared over him,
 Have raised their cries.
 They have made his land a waste,
 His cities desolate, without inhabitants.

[d] I.e. against Jerusalem and Judah
[e] Lit. "the people of the land"

[a] Lit. "shepherds"; cf. 23.1 ff.

JEREMIAH 2·16

16 Those, too, in Noph and Tahpanhes[b]
   [c-]Will lay bare[-c] your head.
17 See, [d-]that is the price you have paid
   For forsaking the LORD your God[-d]
   [c-]While He led you in the way.[-c]
18 What, then, is the good of your going to Egypt
   To drink the waters of the Nile?
   And what is the good of your going to Assyria
   To drink the waters of the Euphrates?
19 Let your misfortune reprove you,
   Let your afflictions rebuke you;
   Mark well how bad and bitter it is
   That you forsake the LORD your God,
   That awe for Me is not in you
             —declares the Lord GOD of Hosts.
20 For long ago you[e] broke your yoke,
   Tore off your yoke-bands,
   And said, "I will not work!"[f]
   On every high hill and under every verdant tree,
   You recline as a whore.
21 I planted you with noble vines,
   All with choicest seed;
   Alas, I find you changed
   Into a base, an alien vine!
22 Though you wash with natron
   And use much lye,
   Your guilt is ingrained before Me
             —declares the Lord GOD.
23 How can you say, "I am not defiled,
   I have not gone after the Baalim"?
   Look at your deeds in the Valley,[g]
   Consider what you have done!
   Like a lustful she-camel,
   [c-]Restlessly running about,[-c]
24 Or like a wild ass used to the desert,
   Snuffing the wind in her eagerness,
   Whose passion none can restrain,
   None that seek her need grow weary—
   In her season, they'll find her!

25 Save your foot from going bare,
   And your throat from thirst.
   But you say, "It is no use.
   No, I love the strangers,[h]
   And after them I must go."
26 Like a thief chagrined when he is caught,
   So is the House of Israel chagrined—
   They, their kings, their officers,
   And their priests and prophets.
27 They said to wood, "You are my father,"
   To stone, "You gave birth to me,"
   While to Me they turned their backs
   And not their faces.
   But in their hour of calamity they cry,
   "Arise and save us!"
28 And where are those gods
   You made for yourself?
   Let them arise and save you, if they can,
   In your hour of calamity.
   For your gods have become, O Judah,
   As many as your towns!
29 Why do you call Me to account?
   You have all rebelled against Me
             —declares the LORD.
30 To no purpose did I smite your children;
   They would not accept correction.
   Your sword has devoured your prophets
   Like a ravening lion.
31 [c-]O generation, behold[-c] the word of the LORD!
   Have I been like a desert to Israel,
   Or like a land of deep gloom?
   Then why do My people say, "We have broken loose,
   We will not come to You any more?"
32 Can a maiden forget her jewels,
   A bride her adornments?
   Yet My people have forgotten Me—
   Days without number.

33 How skillfully you plan your way
   To seek out love!
   Why, you have even taught
   The worst of women your ways.
34 Moreover, on your garments is found
   The lifeblood of the innocent poor—
   You did not catch them breaking in.[i]

---

[b] Cities in Egypt. The Egyptians, like the Assyrians, will prove a disappointment; cf. v. 36
[c-c] Meaning of Heb uncertain
[d-d] Lit. "that is what your forsaking the LORD your God is doing to you"
[e] For the form, cf. *shaqqamti*, Judges 5.7; others "I"
[f] Following the *kethib*; *qere* "transgress"
[g] I.e. of Hinnom; cf. 7.31–32; 32.35
[h] I.e. other gods
[i] In which case there might have been an excuse for killing them; cf. Exod. 22.1

JEREMIAH 2.35

^{c-c}Yet, despite all these things,^{-c}
³⁵ You say, "I have been acquitted;
Surely, His anger has turned away from me."
Lo, I will bring you to judgment
For saying, "I have not sinned."

³⁶ How you cheapen yourself,
By changing your course!
You shall be put to shame through Egypt,
Just as you were put to shame through Assyria.
³⁷ From this way, too, you will come out
^{j-}With your hands on your head;^{-j}
For the LORD has rejected those you trust,
You will not prosper with them.

3

¹ [The word of the LORD came to me] as follows: If a man divorces his wife, and she leaves him and marries another man, can he ever go back to her? Would not such a land be defiled?^a Now you have whored with many lovers: can you return to Me?—says the LORD.

² Look up to the bare heights, and see:
Where have they not lain with you?
You waited for them on the roadside
Like a bandit^b in the wilderness.
And you defiled the land
With your whoring and your debauchery.
³ And when showers were withheld
And the late rains did not come,
You had the brazenness^c of a street woman,
You refused to be ashamed.
⁴ Just now you called to Me, "Father!
You are the Guide of my youth.
⁵ Does one bear a grudge for all time?
Does one hold it forever?"
That is how you spoke;
You did wrong, and ^{d-}had your way.^{-d}

⁶ The LORD said to me in the days of King Josiah: Have you seen what Rebel Israel did, going to every high mountain and under every leafy tree, and whoring there? ⁷ I thought: after she has done all these things, she will come back to Me. But she did not come back; and her sister, Faithless Judah, saw it. ⁸ I noted: because Rebel Israel had committed adultery, I cast her off and handed her a bill of divorce; yet her sister, Faithless Judah, was not afraid—she too went and whored. ⁹ Indeed, the land was defiled by her casual immorality, as she committed adultery with stone and with wood.^e ¹⁰ And after all that, her sister, Faithless Judah, did not return to Me wholeheartedly, but insincerely—declares the LORD.

¹¹ And the LORD said to me: Rebel Israel has shown herself more in the right than Faithless Judah. ¹² Go, make this proclamation toward the north, and say: Turn back, O Rebel Israel—declares the LORD. I will not look on you in anger, for I am compassionate—declares the LORD; I do not bear a grudge for all time. ¹³ Only recognize your sin; for you have transgressed against the LORD, and scattered your favors^f among strangers under every leafy tree, and you have not heeded Me—declares the LORD.

¹⁴ Turn back, rebellious children—declares the LORD. Though I have rejected^g you, I will take you, one from a town and two from a clan, and bring you to Zion. ¹⁵ And I will give you shepherds^h after My own heart, who will pasture you with knowledge and skill.
¹⁶ And when you increase and are fertile in the land, in those days—declares the LORD—men shall no longer speak of the Ark of the Covenant of the LORD, nor shall it come to mind. They shall not mention it, or miss it, or make another. ¹⁷ At that time, they shall call Jerusalem "Throne of the LORD," and all nations shall assemble there, in the name of the LORD at Jerusalem; they shall no longer

---

^{c-c}Meaning of Heb uncertain
^{j-j}A gesture of wild grief; cf. II Sam. 13.19

^aCf. Deut. 24.1–4
^bLit. "Arab"
^cLit. "forehead"
^{d-d}Meaning of Heb uncertain
^eShe deserted her God for idols of stone and wood
^fLit. "ways"
^gTaking *ba'alti* as equivalent to *bahalti*; cf. note at 31.32
^hSee note at 2.8

JEREMIAH 3·18

follow the willfulness of their evil hearts. ¹⁸ In those days, the House of Judah shall go with the House of Israel; they shall come together from the land of the north to the land I gave your fathers as a possession.

¹⁹ I had resolved to adopt you as My child, and I gave you a desirable land—the fairest heritage of all the nations; and I thought you would surely call Me "Father," and never cease to be loyal to Me. ²⁰ Instead, you have broken faith with Me, as a woman breaks faith with a paramour, O House of Israel—declares the Lord.

²¹ Hark! On the bare heights is heard
    The suppliant weeping of the people of Israel,
    For they have gone a crooked way,
    Ignoring the Lord their God.

²² Turn back, O rebellious children,
    I will heal your afflictions!

    "Here we are, we come to You,
    For You, O Lord, are our God!
²³ ⁱ⁻Surely, futility comes from the hills,
    Confusion from the mountains.⁻ⁱ
    Only through the Lord our God
    Is there deliverance for Israel.
²⁴ But the Shameful Thing^j has consumed
    The toil of our fathers ever since our youth—
    Their flocks and herds,
    Their sons and daughters.
²⁵ Let us lie down in our shame,
    Let our disgrace cover us;
    For we have sinned against the Lord our God,
    We and our fathers from our youth to this day,
    And we have not heeded the Lord our God."

¹ If you return, O Israel
                              —declares the Lord—
    If you return to Me,
    If you remove your abominations from My presence
    And do not waver,
² And ^{a-}swear, "As the Lord lives,"^{-a}
    In sincerity, justice, and righteousness—
    Nations shall bless themselves by you^b
    And praise themselves by you.^b

³ For thus said the Lord to the men of Judah and to Jerusalem:
    Break up the untilled ground,
    And do not sow among thorns.
⁴ Open^c yourselves to the Lord,
    Remove the thickening about your hearts—
    Lest My wrath break forth like fire,
    And burn, with none to quench it,
    Because of your wicked acts.

⁵ Proclaim in Judah,
    Announce in Jerusalem,
    And say:
    "Blow the horn in the land!"
    Shout aloud and say:
    "Assemble and let us go
    Into the fortified cities!"
⁶ Set up a signpost: To Zion.
    Take refuge, do not delay!
    For I bring evil from the north,
    And great disaster.
⁷ The lion has come up from his thicket:
    The destroyer of nations has set out,
    Has departed from his place,
    To make your land a desolation;
    Your cities shall be ruined,
    Without inhabitants.
⁸ For this, put on sackcloth,
    Mourn and wail;
    For the blazing anger of the Lord
    Has not turned away from us.
⁹ And in that day
                              —declares the Lord—
    The mind of the king
    And the mind of the nobles shall fail,
    The priests shall be appalled,
    And the prophets shall be aghast.

ⁱ⁻ⁱI.e. the pagan rites celebrated on the hills are futile; exact force of Heb uncertain
^jHeb *Bosheth*, a contemptuous substitute for Baal

^{a-a}I.e. profess the worship of the Lord
^bI.e. Israel; Heb "him"
^cLit. "circumcise"; cf. Deut. 10.16 and 30.6

JEREMIAH 4·10

¹⁰ ᵈ⁻And I said:⁻ᵈ Ah, Lord GOD! Surely You have deceived this people and Jerusalem, saying:
   It shall be well with you—
   Yet the sword threatens the very life!
¹¹ At that time, it shall be said concerning this people and Jerusalem:
   The conduct of ᵉ⁻My poor people⁻ᵉ is like searing wind
   From the bare heights of the desert—
   It will not serve to winnow or to fan.
¹² A full blast from them comes against Me:
   Now I in turn will bring charges against them.

¹³ Lo, heᶠ ascends like clouds,
   His chariots are like a whirlwind,
   His horses are swifter than eagles.
   Woe to us, we are ruined!

¹⁴ Wash your heart clean of wickedness,
   O Jerusalem, that you may be rescued.
   How long will you harbor within you
   Your evil designs?

¹⁵ Hark, one proclaims from Dan
   And announces calamity from Mount Ephraim!
¹⁶ Tell the nations: Here they are!
   Announce concerning Jerusalem:
   Watchersᶠ are coming from a distant land,
   They raise their voices against the towns of Judah.
¹⁷ Like guards of fields, they surround her on every side.
   For she has rebelled against Me
                              —declares the LORD.
¹⁸ Your conduct and your acts
   Have brought this upon you;
   This is your bitter punishment;
   It pierces your very heart.

¹⁹ Oh, my suffering,ᵍ my suffering!
   How I writhe!
   Oh, the walls of my heart!
   My heart moans within me,
   I cannot be silent;
   For ʰ⁻I hear⁻ʰ the blast of a horn,
   The alarm of war.
²⁰ Disaster overtakes disaster,
   For all the land has been ravaged.
   Suddenly my tents have been ravaged,
   In a moment, my tent cloths.
²¹ How long must I see standards
   And hear the blast of a horn?

²² For My people is stupid,
   They give Me no heed;
   They are foolish children,
   They are not intelligent.
   They are clever at doing wrong,
   But unable to do right.

²³ I look at the earth,
   It is unformed and void;
   At the skies,

ᵈ⁻ᵈSeptuagint reads "And they shall say"
ᵉ⁻ᵉLit. "the daughter that is My people"; so frequently in poetry
ᶠI.e. the invader of v. 7
ᵍLit. "entrails"
ʰ⁻ʰLit. "you, O my being, hear"

9

JEREMIAH 4·24

And their light is gone.
24 I look at the mountains,
They are quaking;
And all the hills are rocking.
25 I look: no man is left.
And all the birds of the sky have fled.
26 I look: the farmland is desert,
And all its towns are in ruin—
Because of the LORD,
Because of His blazing anger.
27 (For thus said the LORD:
The whole land shall be desolate,
But I will not make an end of it.)
28 For this the earth mourns,
And skies are dark above—
Because I have spoken, I have planned,
And I will not relent or turn back from it.

29 At the shout of horseman and bowman
The whole city flees.
They enter the thickets,
They clamber up the rocks.
The whole city is deserted,
Not a man remains there.
30 And you, who are doomed to ruin,
What do you accomplish by wearing scarlet,
By decking yourself in jewels of gold,
By enlarging your eyes with kohl?
You beautify yourself in vain:
Lovers despise you,
They seek your life!
31 I hear a voice as of one in travail,
Anguish as of a woman bearing her first child,
The voice of Fair Zion
Panting, stretching out her hands:
"Alas for me! I faint
Before the killers!"

5

1 Roam the streets of Jerusalem,
Search its squares,
Look about and note:
You will not find a man;
There is none who acts justly,
Who seeks integrity—
That I should pardon her.
2 Even when they say, "As the LORD lives,"
They are sure to be swearing falsely.
3 O LORD, Your eyes look for integrity.
You have struck them, but they sensed no pain;
You have consumed them, but they would accept no discipline.
They made their faces harder than rock,
They refused to turn back.

4 Then I thought: These are just poor folk;
They act foolishly;
For they do not know the way of the LORD,
The rules of their God.
5 So I will go to the wealthy
And speak with them:
Surely they know the way of the LORD,
The rules of their God.
But they as well had broken the yoke,
Had snapped the bonds.
6 Therefore,
The lion of the forest strikes them down,
The wolf of the desert ravages them.
A leopard lies in wait by their towns;
Whoever leaves them will be torn in pieces.
For their transgressions are many,
Their rebellious acts unnumbered.

7 Why should I forgive you?
Your children have forsaken Me
And sworn by no-gods.
When I fed them their fill,
They committed adultery
And went trooping to the harlot's house.
8 They were *a*-well-fed, lusty-*a* stallions,
Each neighing at another's wife.
9 Shall I not punish such deeds?
—says the LORD—
Shall I not bring retribution
On a nation such as this?
10 Go up among her vines*b* and destroy;
Lop off her trailing branches,

a-a Meaning of Heb uncertain
b Lit. "rows"

JEREMIAH 5.11

For they are not of the LORD.
(But do not make an end.)

¹¹ For the House of Israel and the House of Judah
Have betrayed Me

—declares the LORD.

¹² They have been false to the LORD
And said: "*c*-It is not so!-*c*
No trouble shall come upon us,
We shall not see sword or famine.
¹³ The prophets are just wind
And the Word is not in them;
Thus-and-thus shall be done to them!"

¹⁴ Assuredly, thus said the LORD,
The God of Hosts:
Because they*d* said that,
I am putting My words into your mouth as fire,
And this people shall be firewood,
Which it will consume.
¹⁵ Lo, I am bringing against you, O House of Israel,
A nation from afar

—declares the LORD;

It is an enduring nation,
It is an ancient nation;
A nation whose language you do not know—
You will not understand what they say.
¹⁶ *e*-Their quivers-*e* are like a yawning grave—
They are all mighty men.
¹⁷ They will devour your harvest and food,
They will devour your sons and daughters,
They will devour your flocks and herds,
They will devour your vines and fig trees.
They will batter down with the sword
The fortified towns on which you rely.

¹⁸ But even in those days—declares the LORD—I will not make an end of you. ¹⁹ And when they*d* ask, "Because of what did the LORD our God do all these things?" you shall answer them, "Because you forsook Me and served alien gods on your own land, you will have to serve foreigners in a land not your own."

²⁰ Proclaim this to the House of Jacob
And announce it in Judah:

²¹ Hear this, O foolish people,
Devoid of intelligence,
That have eyes but can't see,
That have ears but can't hear!
²² Should you not revere Me

—says the LORD—

Should you not tremble before Me,
Who set the sand as a boundary to the sea,
As a limit for all time, not to be transgressed?
Though its waves toss, they cannot prevail;
Though they roar, they cannot pass it.
²³ Yet this people has a wayward and defiant heart;
They have turned aside and gone their way.
²⁴ They have not said to themselves,
"Let us revere the LORD our God,
Who gives the rain,
The early and late rain in season,
Who keeps for our benefit
The weeks appointed for harvest."
²⁵ It is your iniquities that have diverted these things,
Your sins that have withheld the bounty from you.
²⁶ For among My people are found wicked men,
a-Who lurk, like fowlers lying in wait;-*a*
They set up a trap to catch men.
²⁷ As a cage is full of birds,
So their houses are full of guile;
That is why they have grown so wealthy.
²⁸ They have become fat and sleek;
They *f*-pass beyond the bounds of wickedness,-*f*
And they prosper.
They will not judge the case of the orphan,
Nor hear the plea of the needy.
²⁹ Shall I not punish such deeds

—declares the LORD—

Shall I not bring retribution
On a nation such as this?
³⁰ An appalling, horrible thing
Has happened in the land:
³¹ The prophets prophesy falsely,
And the priests *a*-rule accordingly;-*a*
And My people like it so.
But what will you do at the end of it?

---

a-a Meaning of Heb uncertain

c-c Or "Not He"; cf. Deut. 32.39; Isa. 43.13
d Heb "you"
e-e Emendation yields "whose mouths"
f-f Some ancient versions read "have transgressed My words for evil"

6

1 Flee for refuge, O people of Benjamin,
   Out of the midst of Jerusalem!
   Blow the horn in Tekoa,
   Set up a signal at Beth-ha-cherem!
   For evil is appearing from the north,
   And great disaster.
2 ᵃ⁻Fair Zion, the lovely and delicate,
   I shall destroy.⁻ᵃ
3 Against her come shepherds with their flocks,
   They pitch tents all around her;
   Each grazes ᵇ⁻the sheep under his care.⁻ᵇ
4 ᶜ⁻Prepare for⁻ᶜ battle against her:
   "Up! we will attack at noon."
   "Alas for us! for day is declining,
   The shadows of evening grow long."
5 "Up! let us attack by night,
   And wreck her fortresses."

6 For thus said the LORD of Hosts:
   Hew down her trees,
   And raise a siege-mound against Jerusalem.
   ᵈ⁻She is the city destined for punishment;⁻ᵈ
   Only fraud is found in her midst.
7 As a well flows with water,
   So she flows with wickedness.
   Lawlessness and rapine are heard in her;
   Before Me constantly are sickness and wounds.
8 Accept rebuke, O Jerusalem,
   Lest I come to loathe you,
   Lest I make you a desolation,
   An uninhabited land.

9 For thus said the LORD of Hosts:
   Let them glean thoroughly, as a vine,
   The remnant of Israel.
   Pass your hand again,
   Like a vintager,
   Over its branches.

10 ᵉTo whom shall I speak,
   Give warning that they may hear?
   Their ears are blocked
   And they cannot listen.
   See, the word of the LORD has become for them
   An object of scorn; they will have none of it.
11 But I am filled with the wrath of the LORD,
   I cannot hold it in.
   Pour it on the infant in the street,
   And on the company of youths gathered together!

   Yes, men and women alike shall be captured,
   Elders and those of advanced years.
12 Their houses shall pass to others,
   Fields and wives as well,
   For I will stretch out My arm
   Against the inhabitants of the country
                               —declares the LORD.
13 For from the smallest to the greatest,
   They are all greedy for gain;
   Priest and prophet alike,
   They all act falsely.
14 They offer healing offhand
   For the wounds of My people,
   Saying, "All is well, all is well,"
   When nothing is well.
15 They have acted shamefully;
   They have done abhorrent things—
   Yet they do not feel shame,
   And they cannot be made to blush.
   Assuredly, they shall fall among the falling,
   They shall stumble at the time when I deal with them
                               —said the LORD.
16 Thus said the LORD:
   Stand by the roads and consider,
   Inquire about ancient paths:
   Which is the road to happiness?
   Travel it, and find tranquility for yourselves.
   But they said, "We will not."
17 And I raised up watchmenᶠ for you:
   "Hearken to the sound of the horn!"
   But they said, "We will not."
18 Hear well, O nations,
   And know, ᵃ⁻O community, what is in store for them.⁻ᵃ
19 Hear, O earth!
   I am going to bring disaster upon this people,
   The outcome of their own schemes;

ᵃ⁻ᵃMeaning of Heb uncertain
ᵇ⁻ᵇUnderstanding *yado* as in Ps. 95.7
ᶜ⁻ᶜLit. "Consecrate"
ᵈ⁻ᵈEmendation yields "She is the city of falseness"
ᵉThe prophet speaks
ᶠI.e. prophets

JEREMIAH 6·20

For they would not hearken to My words,
And they rejected My Instruction.
20 What need have I of frankincense
That comes from Sheba,
Or fragrant cane from a distant land?
Your burnt offerings are not acceptable
And your sacrifices are not pleasing to Me.
21 Assuredly, thus said the LORD:
I shall put before this people stumbling blocks
Over which they shall stumble—
Fathers and children alike,
Neighbor and friend shall perish.

22 Thus said the LORD:
See, a people comes from the northland,
A great nation is roused
From the remotest parts of the earth.
23 They grasp the bow and javelin;
They are cruel, they show no mercy;
The sound of them is like the roaring sea.
They ride upon horses,
Caparisoned, as a man for war,
Against you, O Fair Zion!

24 "We have heard the report of them,
Our hands fail;
Pain seizes us,
Agony like a woman in childbirth,
25 Do not go out into the country,
Do not walk the roads!
For the sword of the enemy is there,
Terror on every side."

26 ᵍ⁻My poor people,⁻ᵍ
Put on sackcloth
And wallow in the dust!
Mourn, as for an only child;
Wail bitterly,
For suddenly the destroyer
Is coming upon us.

27 I have made you an assayer of My people
—A refinerᵃ—
You are to note and assay their ways.

28 They are copper and iron:
They are all stubbornly defiant;
They ʰ⁻deal basely⁻ʰ—
All of them act corruptly.
29 ᵃ⁻The bellows puffs;
The lead is consumed by fire.⁻ᵃ
Yet the smelter smelts to no purpose—
The drossᵃ is not separated out.
30 They are called "rejected silver,"
For the LORD has rejected them.

7

¹ The word which came to Jeremiah from the LORD: ² Stand at the gate of the House of the LORD, and there proclaim this word. Hear the word of the LORD, all you of Judah who enter these gates to worship the LORD! ³ Thus said the LORD of Hosts, the God of Israel: Mend your ways and your actions, and I will ᵃ⁻let you dwell⁻ᵃ in this place. ⁴ Don't put your trust in illusions and say, "The Temple of the LORD, the Temple of the LORD, the Temple of the LORD are these [buildings]." ⁵ No, if you really mend your ways and your actions; if you execute justice between one man and another; ⁶ if you do not oppress the stranger, the orphan, and the widow; if you do not shed the blood of the innocent in this place; if you do not follow other gods, to your own hurt— ⁷ then only will I ᵃ⁻let you dwell⁻ᵃ in this place, in the land which I gave to your fathers for all time. ⁸ See, you are relying on illusions that are of no avail. ⁹ Will you steal and murder and commit adultery and swear falsely, and sacrifice to Baal, and follow other gods which you have not experienced,ᵇ ¹⁰ and then come and stand before Me in this House which bears My name and say, "We are safe"?—[Safe] to do all these abhorrent things! ¹¹ Do you consider this House, which bears My name, to be a den of thieves? As for Me, I have been watching—declares the LORD.

¹² Just go to My place at Shiloh, where I had estab-

ᵃ⁻ᵃMeaning of Heb uncertain
ᵍ⁻ᵍLit. "Daughter of My people"; so frequently in poetry
ʰ⁻ʰSee note at Lev. 19.15

ᵃ⁻ᵃChange of vocalization yields "dwell with you"; so Aquila and Vulgate
ᵇSee note at Deut. 11.28

JEREMIAH 7·13

lished My name formerly, and see what I did to it because of the wickedness of My people Israel. ¹³ And now, because you do all these things—declares the LORD—and though I spoke to you persistently, you would not listen; and though I called to you, you would not respond— ¹⁴ therefore I will do to the House which bears My name—on which you rely—and to the place which I gave you and your fathers, just what I did to Shiloh. ¹⁵ And I will cast you out of My presence as I cast out your brothers, the whole brood of Ephraim.

¹⁶ As for you, do not pray for this people, do not raise a cry of prayer on their behalf, do not plead with Me; for I will not listen to you. ¹⁷ Don't you see what they are doing in the towns of Judah and in the streets of Jerusalem? ¹⁸ The children gather sticks, the fathers build the fire, and the mothers knead dough, to make cakes for the Queen of Heaven,ᶜ and they pour libations to other gods, to vex Me. ¹⁹ Is it Me they are vexing?—says the LORD. It is rather themselves, to their own disgrace. ²⁰ Assuredly, thus said the Lord GOD: My wrath and My fury will be poured out upon this place, on man and on beast, on the trees of the field and the fruit of the soil. It shall burn, with none to quench it.

²¹ Thus said the LORD of Hosts, the God of Israel: Add your burnt offerings to your other sacrifices and eat the meat! ²² For when I freed your fathers from the land of Egypt, I did not speak with them or command them concerning burnt offerings or sacrifice. ²³ But this is what I commanded them: Do My bidding, that I may be your God and you may be My people; walk only in the way that I enjoin upon you, that it may go well with you. ²⁴ Yet they did not listen or give ear; they followed their own counsels, the willfulness of their evil hearts. They have gone backward, not forward, ²⁵ from the day your fathers left the land of Egypt until today. And though I kept sending all My servants, the prophets, to themᵈ early every day, ²⁶ they would not listen to Me or give ear. They stiffened their necks, they acted worse than their fathers.

²⁷ You shall say all these things to them, but they will not listen to you; you shall call to them, but they will not respond to you. ²⁸ Then say to them: This is the nation that would not obey the LORD their God, that would not accept rebuke. Faithfulness has perished, vanished from their mouths.

²⁹ Shear your locks and cast them away,
Take up a lament on the heights,
For the LORD has spurned and cast off
The brood that provoked His wrath.

³⁰ For the people of Judah have done what displeases Me—declares the LORD. They have set up their abominations in the House which is called by My name, and they have defiled it. ³¹ And they have built the shrines of Topheth in the Valley of Ben-hinnom to burn their sons and daughters in fire—which I never commanded, which never came to My mind.

³² Assuredly, days are coming—declares the LORD —when men shall no longer speak of "Topheth" or "the Valley of Ben-hinnom," but of "the Valley of Massacre"; and they shall bury in Topheth until no room is left. ³³ The carcasses of this people shall be food for the birds of the sky and the beasts of the earth, with none to frighten them off. ³⁴ And I will silence in the towns of Judah and the streets of Jerusalem the sound of mirth and gladness, the voice of bridegroom and bride. For the whole land shall fall to ruin.

¹ At that time—declares the LORD—the bones of the kings of Judah, of its officers, of the priests, of the prophets, and of the inhabitants of Jerusalem shall be taken out of their graves ² and exposed to the sun, the moon, and all the hosts of heaven which they loved and served and followed, to which they turned and bowed down. They shall not be gathered for reburial; they shall become dung upon the face of the earth. ³ And death shall

---
ᶜ I.e. the mother goddess (Ishtar, Astarte) in whose honor these cakes were baked
ᵈ Heb "you"

JEREMIAH 8.4

be preferable to life for all that are left of this wicked folk, in all the other places to which I shall banish them—declares the LORD of Hosts.

4 Say to them: Thus said the LORD:

When men fall, do they not get up again?
If they turn aside, do they not turn back?
5 Why is this people—Jerusalem—rebellious
With a persistent rebellion?
They cling to deceit,
They refuse to return.
6 I have listened and heard:
They do not speak honestly.
No one regrets his wickedness
And says, "What have I done!"
They all persist in their wayward course
Like a steed dashing forward in the fray.
7 Even the stork in the sky knows her seasons,
And the turtledove, swift, and swallow
Keep the time of their coming;
But My people pay no heed
To the law of the LORD.
8 How can you say, "We are wise,
And we possess the Instruction of the LORD"?
Assuredly, for naught has the pen labored,
For naught the scribes!
9 The wise shall be put to shame,
Shall be dismayed and caught;
See, they reject the word of the LORD,
So their wisdom amounts to nothing.

10 Assuredly, I will give their wives to others,
And their fields to dispossessors;
For from the smallest to the greatest,
They are all greedy for gain;
Priest and prophet alike,
They all act falsely.
11 They offer healing offhand
For the wounds of My poor people,
Saying, "All is well, all is well,"
When nothing is well.
12 They have acted shamefully;
They have done abhorrent things—
Yet they do not feel shame,
They cannot be made to blush.
Assuredly, they shall fall among the falling,
They shall stumble at the time of their doom
—said the LORD.
13 a-I will make an end of them-a
—declares the LORD:

No grapes left on the vine,
No figs on the fig tree,
The leaves all withered;
b-Whatever I have given them is gone.-b
14 Why are we sitting by?
Let us gather into the fortified cities
And meet our doom there.
For the LORD our God has doomed us,
He has made us drink a bitter draft,
Because we sinned against the LORD.
15 We hoped for good fortune, but no happiness came;
For a time of relief—instead there is terror!
16 The snorting of their horses was heard from Dan;
At the loud neighing of their steeds
The whole land quaked.
They came and devoured the land and what was in it,
The towns and those who dwelt in them.

17 Lo, I will send serpents against you,
Adders that cannot be charmed,
And they shall bite you
—declares the LORD.
18 b-When in grief I would seek comfort,-b
My heart is sick within me.

19 c-"Is not the LORD in Zion?
Is not her King within her?
Why then did they anger Me with their images,
With alien futilities?"

Hark! The outcry of d-My poor people-d
From the land far and wide:
20 "Harvest is past,
Summer is gone,
But we have not been saved."

---

a-a Meaning of Heb uncertain; change of vocalization yields "Their fruit harvest has been gathered in"
b-b Meaning of Heb uncertain
c Here God is speaking
d-d See note at 4.11

JEREMIAH 8·21

21 By the calamity of my people I am shattered;
   I am dejected, seized by desolation.
22 Is there no balm in Gilead?
   Can no physician be found?
   Why has healing not yet
   Come to my poor people?
23 Oh, that my head were water,
   My eyes a fount of tears!
   Then would I weep day and night
   For the slain of my poor people.

9

1 Oh, to be in the desert,
   At an encampment for wayfarers!
   Oh, to leave my people,
   To go away from them—
   For they are all adulterers,
   A band of rogues.

2 They bend their tongues like bows;
   They are valorous in the land
   For treachery, not for honesty;
   They advance from evil to evil.
   And they do not heed Me
                              —declares the LORD.
3 Beware, every man of his friend!
   Trust not even a brother!
   For every brother takes advantage,
   Every friend *-is base in his dealings.-*
4 One man cheats the other,
   They will not speak truth;
   They have trained their tongues to speak falsely;
   *-They wear themselves out working iniquity.
5 You dwell in the midst of deceit.
   In their deceit,-* they refuse to heed Me
                              —declares the LORD.

6 Assuredly, thus said the LORD of Hosts:
   Lo, I shall smelt and assay them—
   -For what else can I do because of My people?-
7 Their tongue is a sharpened arrow,
   They use their mouths to deceive.
   One speaks to his fellow in friendship,
   But lays an ambush for him in his heart.
8 Shall I not punish them for such deeds?
                              —says the LORD—
   Shall I not bring retribution
   On such a nation as this?

9 For the mountains I take up weeping and wailing,
   For the pastures in the wilderness, a dirge.
   They are laid waste; no man passes through,
   And no sound of cattle is heard.
   Birds of the sky and beasts as well
   Have fled and are gone.

10 I will turn Jerusalem into rubble,
   Into dens for jackals;

a-a See note at Lev. 19.16
b-b Meaning of Heb uncertain

And I will make the towns of Judah
A desolation without inhabitants.

11 What man is so wise
That he understands this?
To whom has the LORD's mouth spoken,
So that he can explain it:
Why is the land in ruins,
Laid waste like a wilderness,
With none passing through?

12 The LORD replied: Because they forsook the Teaching I had set before them. They did not obey Me and they did not follow it, 13 but followed their own willful heart and followed the Baalim, as their fathers had taught them. 14 Assuredly, thus said the LORD of Hosts, the God of Israel: I am going to feed that people wormwood and make them drink a bitter draft. 15 I will scatter them among nations which they and their fathers never knew; and I will dispatch the sword after them until I have consumed them.

16 Thus said the LORD of Hosts:
Listen!
Summon the dirge-singers, let them come;
17 Send for the skilled women, let them come.
Let them quickly start a wailing for us,
That our eyes may run with tears,
Our pupils flow with water.

18 For the sound of wailing
Is heard from Zion:
How we are despoiled!
How greatly we are shamed!
Ah, we must leave our land,
Abandon^c our dwellings!

19 Hear, O women, the word of the LORD,
Let your ears receive the word of His mouth,
And teach your daughters wailing,
And one another lamentation.
20 For death has climbed through our windows,
Has entered our citadels,
To cut off babes from the streets,
Young men from the squares.
21 Speak thus—declares the LORD:

The carcasses of men shall lie
Like dung upon the fields,
Like sheaves behind the reaper,
With none to pick them up.

22 Thus said the LORD:

Let not the wise man glory in his wisdom;
Let not the strong man glory in his strength;
Let not the rich man glory in his riches.
23 But only in this should one glory:
In his earnest devotion to Me.
For I the LORD act with kindness,
Justice, and equity in the world;
For in these I delight
—declares the LORD.

24 Lo, days are coming—declares the LORD—when I will take note of everyone ^d-circumcised in the foreskin:^d 25 of Egypt, Judah, Edom, the Ammonites, Moab, and all the desert dwellers who have the hair of their temples clipped. For all these nations are uncircumcised, but all the House of Israel are ^e-uncircumcised of heart.^e

10

1 Hear the word which the LORD has spoken to you, O House of Israel!
2 Thus said the LORD:

Do not learn to go the way of the nations,
And do not be dismayed by portents in the sky;
Let the nations be dismayed by them!
3 For ^a-the laws of the nations^a are delusions:
For it is the work of a craftsman's hands.
He cuts down a tree in the forest with an ax,

---
^c Lit. "They abandoned"
^d-d Force of Heb uncertain
^e-e I.e. their minds are blocked to God's commandments

^a-a Emendation yields "the objects that the nations fear"

JEREMIAH 10·4

4 He adorns it with silver and gold,
   He fastens it[b] with nails and hammer,
   So that it does not totter.
5 They are like a scarecrow in a cucumber patch,
   They cannot speak.
   They have to be carried,
   For they cannot walk.
   Be not afraid of them, for they can do no harm;
   Nor is it in them to do any good.

6 O Lord, there is none like You!
   You are great and Your name is great in power.
7 Who would not revere You, O King of the nations?
   For that is Your due,
   Since among all the wise of the nations
   And among all their royalty
   There is none like You.
8 But they are both dull and foolish;
   [c-][Their] doctrine is but delusion;[-c]
   It is a piece of wood,
9 Silver beaten flat, that is brought from Tarshish,
   And gold from Uphaz,
   The work of a craftsman and the goldsmith's hands;
   Their clothing is blue and purple,
   All of them are the work of skilled men.
10 But the Lord is truly God:
    He is a living God,
    The everlasting King.
    At His wrath, the earth quakes,
    And the nations cannot withstand His rage.

11 [d]Thus shall you say to them: Let the gods, who did not make heaven and earth, perish from the earth and from under these heavens.

12 He made the earth in His might,
    Established the world in His wisdom,
    And in His understanding stretched out the skies.
13 [e-]When He makes His voice heard,[-e]
    There is a rumbling of water in the skies;
    He makes vapors rise from the end of the earth,
    He makes lightnings for the rain,
    And brings forth wind from His treasuries.
14 Every man is proved dull, without knowledge;
    Every goldsmith is put to shame because of the idol,
    For his molten image is a deceit—
    There is no breath in them.
15 They are delusion, a work of mockery;
    In the hour of their doom, they shall perish.
16 Not like these is the Portion of Jacob;
    For it is He who formed all things,
    And Israel is His very own tribe:
    Lord of Hosts is His name.

17 Gather up your bundle[e] from the ground,
    You who dwell under siege!
18 For thus said the Lord: I will fling away the inhabitants of the land this time: I will harass them so that they shall [f-]feel it.[-f]

19 Woe unto me for my hurt,
    My wound is severe!
    I had thought, "This is but a sickness
    That I can bear."
20 [But] my tent is ravaged,
    All my tent cords are broken.
    My children have gone forth from me
    And are no more.
    No one is left to stretch out my tent
    And hang my tent cloths.
21 For the shepherds[g] are dull
    And they do not seek the Lord:
    Therefore they do not prosper,
    And all their flock is scattered.
22 Hark, a noise! It is coming,
    A great commotion out of the north,
    That the towns of Judah may be made a desolation,
    A haunt of jackals.

23 I know, O Lord, that man's road is not his [to choose],
    That man, as he walks, cannot direct his own steps.
24 Chastise me, O Lord, but yet in measure,
    Not in Your wrath, lest You reduce me to naught.
25 Pour out Your wrath on the nations who have not heeded You,
    Upon the clans that have not invoked Your name.
    For they have devoured Jacob,

---
[b] Heb "them"
[c-c] Meaning of Heb uncertain
[d] This sentence is in Aramaic
[e-e] Lit. "At the sound of His making"
[f-f] Emendation yields "have to leave"
[g] I.e. rulers

Have devoured and consumed him,
And have laid desolate his homesteads.

11

¹ The word which came to Jeremiah from the LORD:

² "Hear the terms of this covenant, and recite them to the men of Judah and the inhabitants of Jerusalem! ³ And say to them, Thus said the LORD, the God of Israel: Cursed be the man who will not obey the terms of this covenant, ⁴ which I enjoined upon your fathers when I freed them from the land of Egypt, the iron crucible, saying, 'Obey Me and observe them,ᵃ just as I command you, that you may be My people and I may be your God'— ⁵ in order to fulfill the oath which I swore to your fathers, to give them a land flowing with milk and honey, as is now the case."
And I responded, "Amen, LORD."

⁶ And the LORD said to me, "Proclaim all these things through the towns of Judah and the streets of Jerusalem: Hear the terms of this covenant, and perform them. ⁷ For I have repeatedly and persistently warned your fathers fromᵇ the time I brought them out of Egypt to this day, saying: Obey My commands. ⁸ But they would not listen or give ear; they all followed the willfulness of their evil hearts. So I have brought upon them all the termsᶜ of this covenant, because they did not do what I commanded them to do."

⁹ The LORD said to me, "A conspiracy exists among the men of Judah and the inhabitants of Jerusalem. ¹⁰ They have returned to the iniquities of their fathers of old, who refused to heed My words. They, too, have followed other gods and served them. The House of Israel and the House of Judah have broken the covenant which I made with their fathers."

¹¹ Assuredly, thus said the LORD:
I am going to bring upon them disaster from which they will not be able to escape. Then they will cry out to me, but I will not listen to them. ¹² And the townsmenᵈ of Judah and the inhabitants of Jerusalem will go and cry out to the gods to which they sacrifice; but they will not be able to rescue them in their time of disaster. ¹³ For your gods have become as many as your towns, O Judah, and you have set up as many altars to Shameᵉ as there are streets in Jerusalem—altars for sacrifice to Baal.

¹⁴ As for you, do not pray for this people, do not raise a cry of prayer on their behalf; for I will not listen when they call to Me on account of their disaster.

¹⁵ Why should My beloved be in My House,
ᶠ⁻Who executes so many vile designs?
The sacral flesh will pass away from you,
For you exult while performing your evil deeds.⁻ᶠ
¹⁶ The LORD named you
"Verdant olive tree,
Fair, with choice fruit."
But with a great roaring sound
He has set it on fire,
And its boughs are broken.ᵍ

¹⁷ The LORD of Hosts, who planted you, has decreed disaster for you, because of the evil wrought by the House of Israel and the House of Judah, who angered Me by sacrificing to Baal.

¹⁸ The LORD informed me, and I knew—
Then You let me see their deeds.
¹⁹ For I was like a docile lamb
Led to the slaughter;
I did not realize
That it was against me
They fashioned their plots:
"Let us destroy the tree with its fruit,ʰ
Let us cut him off from the land of the living,
That his name be remembered no more!"

ᵃI.e. the terms of the covenant
ᵇLit. "at"
ᶜI.e. the punishments prescribed for violation
ᵈLit. "towns"
ᵉSee note at 3.24
ᶠ⁻ᶠMeaning of Heb uncertain. Emendation yields "Who does such vile deeds? / Can your treacheries be canceled by sacral flesh / That you exult while performing your evil deeds?"
ᵍEmendation yields "burned"
ʰOr "sap"

JEREMIAH 11·20

20 O LORD of Hosts, O just Judge,
  Who test the thoughts and the mind,
  Let me see Your retribution upon them,
  For I lay my case before You.

21 Assuredly, thus said the LORD of Hosts concerning the men of Anathoth who seek your life and say, "You must not prophesy any more in the name of the LORD, or you will die by our hand"— 22 Assuredly, thus said the LORD of HOSTS: "I am going to deal with them: the young men shall die by the sword, their boys and girls shall die by famine. 23 No remnant shall be left of them, for I will bring disaster on the men of Anathoth, the year of their doom."

12

1 You will win,[a] O LORD, if I make claim against You,
  Yet I shall present charges against You:
  Why does the way of the wicked prosper?
  Why are the workers of treachery at ease?
2 You have planted them, and they have taken root,
  They spread, they even bear fruit.
  You are present in their mouths,
  But far from their thoughts.
3 Yet You, LORD, have noted and observed me;
  You have tested my heart, and found it with You.
  Drive them out like sheep to the slaughter,
  Prepare them for the day of slaying!

4 How long must the land languish,
  And the grass of all the countryside dry up?
  Must beasts and birds perish,
  Because of the evil of its inhabitants,
  Who say, "He will not look upon our future"?[b]

5 [c]If you race with the foot-runners and they exhaust you,
  How then can you compete with horses?
  If you are [d-]secure only[-d] in a tranquil land,
  How will you fare in the jungle of the Jordan?
6 For even your kinsmen and your father's house,
  Even they are treacherous toward you,
  They cry after you as a mob.
  Do not believe them
  When they speak cordially to you.

7 I have abandoned My House,
  I have deserted My possession,
  I have given over My dearly beloved
  Into the hands of her enemies.
8 My own people[e] acted toward Me
  Like a lion in the forest;
  She raised her voice against Me—
  Therefore I have rejected her.
9 [f-]My own people acts toward Me
  Like a bird of prey [or] a hyena;
  Let the birds of prey surround her![-f]
  Go, gather all the wild beasts,
  Bring them to devour!

10 Many shepherds have destroyed My vineyard,
  Have trampled My field,
  Have made My delightful field
  A desolate wilderness.
11 [g-]They have[-g] made her a desolation;
  Desolate, she pours out grief to Me.
  The whole land is laid desolate,
  But no man gives it thought.
12 Spoilers have come
  Upon all the bare heights of the wilderness.
  For a sword of the LORD devours
  From one end of the land to the other;
  No flesh is safe.
13 They have sown wheat and reaped thorns,
  They have endured pain to no avail.
  Be shamed, then, by your harvest—
  By the blazing wrath of the LORD!

14 Thus said the LORD: As for My wicked neighbors who encroach on the heritage which I gave to My people Israel—I am going to uproot them from their soil, and I will uproot the House of Judah

---

[a] Lit. "be in the right"
[b] Septuagint reads "ways"
[c] God here replies to Jeremiah's plea in vv. 1–3
[d-d] Some Septuagint mss. read "not secure"
[e] Lit. "possession"; the land as well as the people, as is clear in v. 14
[f-f] Meaning of Heb uncertain
[g-g] Heb "He has"

out of the midst of them. ¹⁵ Then, after I have uprooted them, I will take them back into favor, and restore them each to his own inheritance and his own land. ¹⁶ And if they learn the ways of My people, to swear by My name—"As the LORD lives"—just as they once taught My people to swear by Baal, then they shall be ʰ⁻built up in the midst of⁻ʰ My people. ¹⁷ But if they do not give heed, I will tear out that nation, tear it out and destroy it—declares the LORD.

13

¹ Thus the LORD said to me: "Go buy yourself a loincloth of linen, and put it around your loins, but do not dip it into water." ² So I bought the loincloth in accordance with the LORD's command, and put it about my loins. ³ And the word of the LORD came to me a second time: ⁴ "Take the loincloth which you bought, which is about your loins, and go at once to Perathᵃ and cover it up there in a cleft of the rock." ⁵ I went and buried it at Perath, as the LORD had commanded me. ⁶ Then, after a long time, the LORD said to me, "Go at once to Perath and take there the loincloth which I commanded you to bury there." ⁷ So I went to Perath and dug up the loincloth from the place where I had buried it; and now the loincloth was ruined; it was not good for anything.

⁸ The word of the LORD came to me: ⁹ Thus said the LORD: Even so will I ruin the overweening pride of Judah and Jerusalem. ¹⁰ This wicked people who refuse to heed My bidding, who follow the willfulness of their own hearts, who follow other gods and serve them and worship them, shall become like that loincloth, which is not good for anything. ¹¹ For as the loincloth clings close to the loins of a man, so I brought close to Me the whole House of Israel and the whole House of Judah—declares the LORD—that they might be My people, for fame, and praise, and splendor. But they would not obey.

¹² And speak this word to them: Thus said the LORD, the God of Israel: "Every jar should be filled with wine." And when they say to you, "Don't we know that every jar should be filled with wine?" ¹³ say to them, "Thus said the LORD: I am going to fill with drunkenness all the inhabitants of this land, and the kings who sit on the throne of David, and the priests and the prophets, and all the inhabitants of Jerusalem. ¹⁴ And I will smash them one against the other, parents and children alike—declares the LORD; no pity, compassion, or mercy will stop Me from destroying them."

¹⁵ Attend and give ear; be not haughty,
    For the LORD has spoken.
¹⁶ Give honor to the LORD your God
    Before He brings darkness,
    Before your feet stumble
    On the mountains in shadow—
    When you hope for light,
    And it is turned to darkness
    And becomes deep gloom.
¹⁷ For if you will not give heed,
    My inmost self must weep,
    Because of your arrogance;
    My eye must stream and flow
    With copious tears,
    Because the flock of the LORD
    Is taken captive.

¹⁸ Say to the king and the queen mother,
    "Sit in a lowly spot;
    For your diadems are abased,
    Your glorious crowns."
¹⁹ The cities of the Negeb are shut,
    There is no one to open them;
    ᵇ⁻Judah is exiled completely,
    All of it exiled.⁻ᵇ
²⁰ Raise your eyes and behold
    Those who come from the north:
    Where are the sheep entrusted to you,
    The flock you took pride in?

ʰ⁻ʰOr "incorporated into"

ᵃOr "the Euphrates"; cf. "Parah," Josh. 18.23
ᵇ⁻ᵇI.e. most of Judah has been annexed by an alien people

JEREMIAH 13·21

21 ᶜ⁻What will you say when they appoint as your heads
   Those among you whom you trained to be tame?⁻ᶜ
   Shall not pangs seize you
   Like a woman in childbirth?
22 And when you ask yourself,
   "Why have these things befallen me?"
   It is because of your great iniquity
   That your skirts are lifted up,
   Your shame exposed.

23 Can the Ethiopian change his skin,
   Or the leopard his spots?
   Just as much can you do good,
   Who are practiced in doing evil!
24 So I will scatter youᵈ like straw that flies
   Before the desert wind.
25 This shall be your lot,
   Your measured portion from Me
                    —declares the LORD.
   Because you forgot Me
   And trusted in falsehood,
26 I in turn will lift your skirts over your face
   And your shame shall be seen.
27 I behold your adulteries,
   Your lustful neighing,
   Your unbridled depravity, your vile acts
   On the hills of the countryside.
   Woe to you, O Jerusalem,
   Who will not be clean!
   How much longer shall it be?

14

¹ The word of the LORD which came to Jeremiah concerning the droughts.

2 Judah is in mourning,
   Her settlements languish.
   Men are bowed to the ground,
   And the outcry of Jerusalem rises.
3 Their nobles sent their servants for water;
   They came to the cisterns, they found no water.
   They returned, their vessels empty.
   They are shamed and humiliated,
   They cover their heads.
4 ᵃ⁻Because of the ground there is dismay,⁻ᵃ
   For there has been no rain on the earth.
   The plowmen are shamed,
   They cover their heads.
5 Even the hind in the field
   Forsakes her newborn fawn,
   Because there is no grass.
6 And the wild asses stand on the bare heights,
   Snuffing the air like jackals;
   Their eyes pine,
   Because there is no herbage.

7 Though our iniquities testify against us,
   Act, O LORD, for the sake of Your name;
   Though our rebellions are many
   And we have sinned against You.
8 O Hope of Israel,
   Its deliverer in time of trouble,
   Why are You like a stranger in the land,
   Like a traveler who stops only for the night?
9 Why are You like a man who is stunned,
   Like a warrior who cannot give victory?
   Yet You are in our midst, O LORD,
   And Your name is attached to us—
   Do not forsake us!

10 Thus said the LORD concerning this people: "Truly, they love to stray, they have not restrained their feet; so the LORD has no pleasure in them. Now He will recall their iniquity and punish their sin."
11 And the LORD said to me, "Do not pray for the benefit of this people. 12 When they fast, I will not listen to their outcry; and when they present burnt offering and meal offering, I will not accept them. I will exterminate them by war, famine, and disease."
13 I said, "Ah, Lord GOD! The prophets are saying to them, 'You shall not see the sword, famine shall not come upon you, but I will give you unfailing security in this place.'"

ᶜ⁻ᶜMeaning of Heb uncertain
ᵈHeb "them"

ᵃ⁻ᵃMeaning of Heb uncertain

JEREMIAH 14·14

¹⁴ The Lord replied: It is a lie that the prophets utter in My name. I have not sent them nor commanded them. I have not spoken to them. A lying vision, an empty divination, the deceit of their own contriving—that is what they prophesy to you! ¹⁵ Assuredly, thus said the Lord concerning the prophets who prophesy in My name though I have not sent them, and who say, "Sword and famine shall not befall this land." Those very prophets shall perish by sword and famine. ¹⁶ And the people to whom they prophesy shall be left lying in the streets of Jerusalem because of the famine and the sword, with none to bury them—they, their wives, their sons, and their daughters. I will pour out upon them [the requital of] their wickedness.

¹⁷ And do you speak to them thus:
Let my eyes run with tears,
Day and night let them not cease,
For ᵇ⁻my hapless peopleᵇ has suffered
A grievous injury, a very painful wound.
¹⁸ If I go out to the country—
Lo, the slain of the sword.
If I enter the city—
Lo, ᶜ⁻those who are sick withᶜ famine.
Both priest and prophet roamᵈ the land,
They know not where.

¹⁹ Have You, then, rejected Judah?
Have You spurned Zion?
Why have You smitten us
So that there is no cure?
Why do we hope for happiness,
But find no good;
For a time of healing,
And meet terror instead?
²⁰ We acknowledge our wickedness, O Lord—
The iniquity of our fathers—
For we have sinned against You.
²¹ For Your name's sake, do not disown us;
Do not dishonor Your glorious throne.
Remember, do not annul Your covenant with us.
²² Can any of the false gods of the nations give rain?
Can the skies of themselves give showers?
Only You can, O Lord our God!

So we hope in You,
For only You made all these things.

15

¹ The Lord said to me, "Even if Moses and Samuel were to ᵃ⁻intercede with Me,⁻ᵃ I would not be won over to that people. Dismiss them from My presence, and let them go forth! ² And if they ask you, 'To what shall we go forth?' answer them, 'Thus said the Lord:

Those destined for the plague, to the plague;
Those destined for the sword, to the sword;
Those destined for famine, to famine;
Those destined for captivity, to captivity.

³ And I will appoint over them four kindsᵇ [of punishment]—declares the Lord—the sword to slay, the dogs to drag, the birds of the sky, and the beasts of the earth to devour and destroy. ⁴ I will make them a horror to all the kingdoms of the earth, on account of King Manasseh son of Hezekiah of Judah, and of what he did in Jerusalem.'"

⁵ But who will pity you, O Jerusalem,
Who will console you?
Who will turn aside to inquire
About your welfare?
⁶ You cast Me off
—declares the Lord—
You go ever backward.
So I have stretched out My hand to destroy you;
I cannot relent.
⁷ I will scatter them as with a winnowing fork
Through the settlements of the earth.
I will bereave, I will destroy My people,
For they would not turn back from their ways.
⁸ Their widows shall be more numerous
Than the sands of the seas.
I will bring against them—
ᶜ⁻Young men and mothers togetherᶜ—
A destroyer at noonday.

ᵇ⁻ᵇ Lit. "the maiden daughter, My people"
ᶜ⁻ᶜ Lit. "the sicknesses of"

ᵃ⁻ᵃ Lit. "stand before Me," as Jeremiah is doing now; cf. 18.20
ᵇ Lit. "clans." Emendation yields "judgments"; cf. Ezek. 14.21
ᶜ⁻ᶜ Exact meaning of Heb uncertain

JEREMIAH 15.9

I will bring down suddenly upon them
Alarm[e] and terror.
9 She who bore seven is forlorn,
Utterly disconsolate;
Her sun has set while it is still day,
She is shamed and humiliated.
The remnant of them I will deliver to the sword,
To the power of their enemies
—declares the LORD.

10 Woe is me, my mother, that you ever bore me—
A man of conflict and strife with all the land!
I never lent to them
And they never lent to me,
Yet everyone curses me.

11 The LORD said:
[c-]Surely, a mere remnant of you
Will I spare for a better fate![-c]
By the enemy [d-]from the north[-d]
In a time of distress and a time of disaster,
Surely, I will have you struck down!
12 [e-]Can iron break iron and bronze?[-e]
13 [f]I will hand over your wealth and your treasures
As a spoil, free of charge,
Because of all your sins throughout your territory.
14 And I will bring your enemies
By way of a land you have not known.
For a fire has flared in My wrath,
It blazes against you.

15 You know, O LORD—
Remember me and take thought of me,
And avenge me on those who persecute me;
[g-]Do not let me perish[-g]
As a result of Your patience![h]
Consider how I have borne insult
On Your account.
16 When Your words were offered, I devoured them;
Your word brought me the delight
And the joy of my heart
That Your name is attached to me,
O LORD, God of Hosts.
17 I have not sat in the company of revelers
And made merry!
I have sat lonely because of Your hand upon me,
For You have filled me with gloom.
18 Why must my pain be endless,
My wound incurable,
Resistant to healing?
You have been to me like a spring that fails,
Like waters that cannot be relied on.

19 Assuredly, thus said the LORD:
If you turn back, I shall take you back
And you shall stand before Me;
If you produce what is noble
[i-]Rather than[-i] worthless,
You shall be My spokesman.
They shall come back to you,
Not you to them.
20 Against this people I will make you
As a fortified wall of bronze:
They will attack you,
But they shall not overcome you,
For I am with you to deliver and save you
—declares the LORD.
21 I will save you from the hands of the wicked
And rescue you from the clutches of the violent.

16

1 The word of the LORD came to me: 2 You are not to marry and not to have sons and daughters in this place. 3 For thus said the LORD concerning any sons and daughters that may be born in this place, and concerning the mothers who bear them, and concerning the fathers who beget them in this land: 4 They shall die gruesome deaths. They shall not be lamented or buried; they shall be like dung on the surface of the ground. They shall be consumed by the sword and by famine, and their corpses shall be food for the birds of the sky and the beasts of the earth.

[c-c] Exact meaning of Heb uncertain
[d-d] Moved up from v. 12 for clarity
[e-e] Emendation yields "He shall shatter iron—iron and bronze!"
[f] Meaning of v. uncertain; vv. 13–14 are substantially repeated in 17.3–4, where Heb text is clear
[g-g] Lit. "Do not take me away"
[h] I.e. Your patience with my persecutors
[i-i] Or "Out of the"

JEREMIAH 16·5

5 For thus said the LORD:

Do not enter a house of mourning,^a
Do not go to lament and to condole with them;
For I have withdrawn My favor from that people
—declares the LORD—
My kindness and compassion.
6 Great and small alike shall die in this land,
They shall not be buried; men shall not lament them,
Nor gash and tonsure themselves for them.
7 They shall not break bread^b for a mourner^c
To comfort him for a bereavement,
Nor offer one a cup of consolation
For the loss of his father or mother.
8 Nor shall you enter a house of feasting,
To sit down with them to eat and drink.

9 For thus said the LORD of Hosts, the God of Israel: I am going to banish from this place, in your days and before your eyes, the sound of mirth and gladness, the voice of bridegroom and bride. 10 And when you announce all these things to that people, and they ask you, "Why has the LORD decreed upon us all this fearful evil? What is the iniquity and what the sin that we have committed against the LORD our God?" 11 say to them, "Because your fathers deserted Me—declares the LORD—and followed other gods and served them and worshiped them; they deserted Me and did not keep My Instructions. 12 And you have acted worse than your fathers, every one of you following the willfulness of his evil heart and paying no heed to Me. 13 Therefore I will hurl you out of this land to a land which neither you nor your fathers have known, and there you will serve other gods, night and day; for I will show you no mercy."

14 Assuredly, days are coming—declares the LORD —when it will no more be said, "As the LORD lives who brought the Israelites out of the land of Egypt," 15 but rather, "As the LORD lives who brought the Israelites out of the northland, and out of all the lands to which He had banished them." For I will bring them back to their land, which I gave to their fathers.

16 Lo, I am sending for many fishermen
—declares the LORD—
And they shall haul them out;
And after that I will send for many hunters,
And they shall hunt them
Out of every mountain and out of every hill
And out of the clefts of the rocks.
17 For My eyes are on all their ways,
They are not hidden from My presence,
Their iniquity is not concealed from My sight.
18 I will pay them in full—
Nay, doubly for their iniquity and their sins—
Because they have defiled My land
With the corpses of their abominations,^d
And have filled My own possession
With their abhorrent things.

19 O LORD, my strength and my stronghold,
My refuge in a day of trouble,
To You nations shall come
From the ends of the earth and say:
Our fathers inherited utter delusions,
Things that are futile and worthless.
20 Can a man make gods for himself?
No-gods are they!
21 Assuredly, I will teach them,
Once and for all I will teach them
My power and My might.
And they shall learn that My name is LORD.

17

1 The guilt of Judah is inscribed
With a stylus of iron,
Engraved with an adamant point
On the tablet of their hearts,
^{a-}And on the horns of their altars,
2 While their children remember^{-a}
Their altars and sacred posts,
By verdant trees,
Upon lofty hills.

^aLit. "religious gathering"
^bSo a few mss. Most mss. and editions read "to them"
^cLit. "mourning"
^dI.e. their lifeless idols

^{a-a}Meaning of Heb uncertain. Emendation yields "Surely the horns of their altars / Are as a memorial against them"

JEREMIAH 17·3

3 [b-]Because of the sin of your shrines
 Throughout your borders,
 I will make your rampart a heap in the field,
 And all your treasures a spoil.[-b]
4 [c-]You will forfeit,[-c] by your own act,
 The inheritance I have given you;
 I will make you a slave to your enemies
 In a land you have never known.
 For you have kindled the flame of My wrath
 Which shall burn for all time.

5 Thus said the LORD:
 Cursed is he who trusts in man,
 Who makes mere flesh his strength,
 And turns his thoughts from the LORD.
6 He shall be like a bush[d] in the desert,
 Which does not sense the coming of good:
 It is set in the scorched places of the wilderness,
 In a barren land without inhabitant.
7 Blessed is he who trusts in the LORD,
 Whose trust is the LORD alone.
8 He shall be like a tree planted by waters,
 Sending forth its roots by a stream:
 It does not sense the coming of heat,
 Its leaves are ever fresh;
 It has no care in a year of drought,
 It does not cease to yield fruit.

9 Most devious is the heart;
 Perverse it is—who can fathom it?
10 I the LORD probe the heart,
 Search the mind—
 To repay every man according to his ways,
 With the proper fruit of his deeds.

11 [b-]Like a partridge hatching what she did not lay,[-b]
 So is one who amasses wealth by unjust means;
 In the middle of his life it will leave him,
 And in the end he will be proved a fool.

12 O Throne of Glory exalted from of old,
 Our Sacred Shrine!
13 O Hope of Israel! O LORD!
 All who forsake You shall be put to shame,
 Those in the land who turn from You[e]
 Shall be doomed[f] men,
 For they have forsaken the LORD,
 The Fount of living waters.

14 Heal me, O LORD, and let me be healed;
 Save me, and let me be saved;
 For You are my glory.

15 See, they say to me:
 "Where is the prediction of the LORD?
 Let it come to pass!"
16 But I have not [g-]evaded
 Being a shepherd in your service,[-g]
 Nor have I longed for the fatal day.
 You know the utterances of my lips,
 They were ever before You.
17 Do not be a cause of dismay to me;
 You are my refuge in a day of calamity.
18 Let my persecutors be shamed,
 And let not me be shamed;
 Let them be dismayed,
 And let not me be dismayed.
 Bring on them the day of disaster,
 And shatter them with double destruction.

19 Thus said the LORD to me: Go and stand in the People's Gate, by which the kings of Judah enter and by which they go forth, and in all the gates of Jerusalem, 20 and say to them: Hear the word of the LORD, O kings of Judah, and all Judah, and all the inhabitants of Jerusalem who enter by these gates! 21 Thus said the LORD: Guard yourselves for your own sake against carrying burdens[h] on the sabbath day, and bringing them through the gates of Jerusalem. 22 Nor shall you carry out burdens from your houses on the sabbath day, or do any work, but you shall hallow the sabbath day, as I commanded your fathers. 23 (But they would not listen or turn their ear; they

---

[b-b] Meaning of Heb uncertain
[c-c] Meaning of Heb uncertain. Emendation yields "Your hand must let go"; cf. Deut. 15.3
[d] Or "tamarisk"; exact meaning of Heb uncertain
[e] Lit. "Me"
[f] Lit. "inscribed"; meaning of line uncertain
[g-g] Exact force of Heb uncertain. Emendation yields "urged you to [bring] misfortune"
[h] Or "merchandise"

JEREMIAH 17·24

stiffened their necks and would not pay heed or accept discipline.) ²⁴ If you obey Me—declares the Lord—and do not bring in burdens through the gates of this city on the sabbath day, but hallow the sabbath day and do no work on it, ²⁵ then through the gates of this city shall enter kings who sit upon the throne of David, with their officers—riding on chariots and horses, they and their officers —and the men of Judah and the inhabitants of Jerusalem. And this city shall be inhabited for all time. ²⁶ And people shall come from the towns of Judah and from the environs of Jerusalem, and from the land of Benjamin, and from the Shephelah, and from the hill country, and from the Negeb, bringing burnt offerings and sacrifices, meal offerings and frankincense, and bringing offerings of thanksgiving to the House of the Lord. ²⁷ But if you do not obey My command to hallow the sabbath day and to carry in no burdens through the gates of Jerusalem on the sabbath day, then I will set fire to its gates; it shall consume the ramparts of Jerusalem and it shall not be extinguished.

18

¹ The word which came to Jeremiah from the Lord: ² "Go down to the house of a potter, and there I will impart My words to you." ³ So I went down to the house of a potter, and found him working at the wheel. ⁴ ᵃ⁻And if the vessel he was making was spoiled, as happens to clay in the potter's hands,⁻ᵃ he would make it into another vessel, such as the potter saw fit to make.

⁵ Then the word of the Lord came to me: ⁶ O House of Israel, can I not deal with you like this potter?—declares the Lord. Just like clay in the hands of the potter, so are you in My hands, O House of Israel! ⁷ At one moment I may decree that a nation or a kingdom shall be uprooted and pulled down and destroyed; ⁸ but if that nation against which I made the decree turns back from its wickedness, I change My mind concerning the punishment I planned to bring on it. ⁹ At another moment I may decree that a nation or a kingdom shall be built and planted; ¹⁰ but if it does evil in My sight and does not obey Me, then I change My mind concerning the good I planned to bestow upon it.

¹¹ And now, say to the men of Judah and the inhabitants of Jerusalem: Thus said the Lord: I am devising*ᵇ* punishment for you and laying plans against you. Turn back, each of you from your wicked ways, and mend your ways and your actions! ¹² But they will say, "It is no use. We will keep on following our own plans; each of us will act in the willfulness of his evil heart."

¹³ Assuredly, thus said the Lord:
 Inquire among the nations:
 Who has heard anything like this?
 Fair Israel has done
 A most horrible thing.
¹⁴ ᶜDoes one forsake Lebanon snow
 From the mountainous rocks?
 Does one abandon cool water
 Flowing from afar?
¹⁵ Yet My people have forgotten Me:
 They sacrifice to a delusion:
 They are made to stumble in their ways—
 The ancient paths—
 And to walk instead on byways,
 On a road not built up.
¹⁶ So their land will become a desolation,
 An object of hissing*ᵈ* for all time.
 Every passerby will be appalled
 And will shake his head.*ᵈ*
¹⁷ Like the east wind, I will scatter them
 Before the enemy.
 ᵉ⁻I will look upon their back, not their face,⁻ᵉ
 In their day of disaster.

¹⁸ They said,ᶠ "Come let us devise a plot against Jeremiah—for instruction shall not fail from the

---

ᵃ⁻ᵃSo some mss. and one early edition. Most mss. and editions read "And if the vessel that he was making with clay in the potter's hands was spoiled"
ᵇThe same Hebrew word as is used above for "potter"
ᶜMeaning of v. uncertain; cf. 2.13, 17.13
ᵈThese actions were performed at the sight of ruin to ward off a like fate from the observer; cf. Lam. 2.15
ᵉ⁻ᵉChange of vocalization yields "I will show them [My] back and not [My] face"
ᶠCf. 20.10

JEREMIAH 18·19

priest, nor counsel from the wise, nor the word from the prophet. Come, let us strike him with the tongue, and we shall no longer have to listen to all those words of his."

19 Listen to me, O Lord—
And note $^{g\text{-}}$what my enemies say!$^{\text{-}g}$
20 Should good be repaid with evil?
Yet they have dug a pit for me.
Remember how I stood before You
To plead in their behalf,
To turn Your anger away from them!
21 Oh, give their children over to famine,
Mow them down by the sword.
Let their wives be bereaved
Of children and husbands,
Let their men be struck down by the plague,
And their young men be slain in battle by the sword.
22 Let an outcry be heard from their houses
When You bring sudden marauders against them;
For they have dug a pit to trap me,
And laid snares for my feet.
23 O Lord, You know
All their plots to kill me.
Do not pardon their iniquity,
Do not blot out their guilt from Your presence.
Let them be made to stumble before You—
Act against them in Your hour of wrath!

19

¹ Thus said the Lord: Go buy a jug of potter's ware. And [take] some of the elders of the people and the priests, ² and go out to the Valley of Ben-hinnom—$^{a\text{-}}$at the entrance of the Harsith Gate$^{\text{-}a}$—and proclaim there the words which I will speak to you. ³ Say:

"Hear the word of the Lord, O Kings of Judah and inhabitants of Jerusalem! Thus said the Lord of Hosts, the God of Israel: I am going to bring such disaster upon this place that the ears of all who hear about it will tingle. ⁴ For they and their fathers and the kings of Judah have forsaken Me, and have made this place alien [to Me]; they have sacrificed in it to other gods whom they have not experienced,^{b} and they have filled this place with the blood of the innocent. ⁵ They have built shrines to Baal, to put their children to the fire as burnt offerings to Baal—which I never commanded, never decreed, and which never came to My mind. ⁶ Assuredly, a time is coming—declares the Lord—when this place shall no longer be called Topheth or Valley of Ben-hinnom, but Valley of Slaughter. ⁷ And I will frustrate^c the plans of Judah and Jerusalem in this place. I will cause them to fall by the sword before their enemies, by the hand of those who seek their lives; and I will give their carcasses as food to the birds of the sky and the beasts of the earth. ⁸ And I will make this city an object of horror and hissing;^{d} everyone who passes by it will be appalled and will hiss over all its wounds. ⁹ And I will cause them to eat the flesh of their sons and the flesh of their daughters, and they shall devour one another's flesh—because of the desperate straits to which they will be reduced by their enemies, who seek their life."

¹⁰ Then you shall smash the jug in the sight of the men who go with you, ¹¹ and say to them: "Thus said the Lord of Hosts: So will I smash this people and this city, as one smashes a potter's vessel, which can never be mended. And they shall bury their dead in Topheth until no room is left for burying. ¹² That is what I will do to this place and its inhabitants—declares the Lord. I will make this city like Topheth: ¹³ the houses of Jerusalem and the houses of the kings of Judah shall be unclean, like that place Topheth—all the houses on the roofs of which offerings were made to the whole host of heaven and libations poured out to other gods."

¹⁴ When Jeremiah returned from Topheth, where the Lord had sent him to prophesy, he stood in the court of the House of the Lord and said to all the people: ¹⁵ "Thus said the Lord of Hosts, the God of Israel: I am going to bring upon this city and

---

$^{g\text{-}g}$Emendation yields "my plea"

$^{a\text{-}a}$Others "by way of the Potsherd Gate"; meaning of Heb uncertain
^{b}See note at Deut. 11.28
^{c}Lit. "empty," Heb *u-baqqothi*, a play on *baqbuq*, "jug" in v. 1
^{d}See note at 18.16

JEREMIAH 20·1

upon all its villages all the disaster which I have decreed against it, for they have stiffened their necks and refused to heed My words."

20

¹ Pashhur son of Immer, the priest who was chief officer of the House of the Lord, heard Jeremiah prophesy these things. ² Pashhur thereupon had Jeremiah flogged and put in the cell[a] at the Upper Benjamin Gate in the House of the Lord. ³ The next day, Pashhur released Jeremiah from the cell.
But Jeremiah said to him, "The Lord has named you not Pashhur, but Magor-missabib.[b] ⁴ For thus said the Lord: I am going to deliver you and all your friends over to terror: they will fall by the sword, while you look on. I will deliver all Judah into the hands of the king of Babylon; he will exile them to Babylon or put them to the sword. ⁵ And I will deliver all the wealth, all the riches, and all the prized possessions of this city, and I will also deliver all the treasures of the kings of Judah into the hands of their enemies: they shall seize them as plunder and carry them off to Babylon. ⁶ As for you, Pashhur, and all who live in your house, you shall go into captivity. You shall come to Babylon; there you shall die and there you shall be buried, and so shall all your friends to whom you prophesied falsely."

⁷ You enticed me, O Lord, and I was enticed;
  You overpowered me and You prevailed.
  I have become a constant laughingstock,
  Everyone jeers at me.
⁸ For every time I speak, I must cry out,
  Must shout, "Lawlessness and rapine!"
  For the word of the Lord causes me
  Constant disgrace and contempt.
⁹ I thought, "I will not mention Him,
  No more will I speak in His name"—
  But [His word] was like a raging fire in my heart,
  Shut up in my bones;
  I could not hold it in, I was helpless.
¹⁰ I heard the whispers of the crowd—
  Terror all around:
  "Inform! Let us inform against him!"
  Every man who is supposed to be my friend
  Is waiting for me to stumble:
  "Perhaps he can be entrapped,
  And we can prevail against him
  And take our vengeance on him."
¹¹ But the Lord is with me like a mighty warrior;
  Therefore my persecutors shall stumble;
  They shall not prevail and shall not succeed.
  They shall be utterly shamed
  With a humiliation for all time,
  Which shall not be forgotten.
¹² O Lord of Hosts, You who test the righteous,
  Who examine the heart and the mind,
  Let me see Your retribution upon them,
  For I lay my case before You.
¹³ Sing unto the Lord,
  Praise the Lord,
  For He has rescued the needy
  From the hands of evildoers!

¹⁴ Accursed be the day
  That I was born!
  Let not the day be blessed
  When my mother bore me!
¹⁵ Accursed be the man
  Who brought my father the news
  And said, "A boy
  Is born to you,"
  And gave him such joy!
¹⁶ Let that man[c] become like the cities
  Which the Lord overthrew without relenting!
  Let him hear shrieks in the morning
  And battle shouts at noontide—
¹⁷ Because he did not kill me before birth
  So that my mother might be my grave,
  And her womb big [with me] for all time.
¹⁸ Why did I ever issue from the womb,
  To see misery and woe,
  To spend all my days in shame!

[a] Meaning of Heb uncertain
[b] I.e. "Terror all around"; cf. v. 10
[c] Emendation yields "day"

21

¹ The word which came to Jeremiah from the LORD, when King Zedekiah sent to him Pashhur son of Malchiah and Zephaniah the priest, son of Maaseiah, to say, ² "Please inquire of the LORD on our behalf, for King Nebuchadrezzar of Babylon has opened war against us. Perhaps the LORD will act for our sake in accordance with all His wonders, so that [Nebuchadrezzar] will withdraw from us."

³ Jeremiah answered them, "Thus shall you say to Zedekiah: ⁴ Thus said the LORD, the God of Israel: I am going to turn around the weapons in your hands with which you are battling outside the wall against those who are besieging you—the king of Babylon and the Chaldeans. I will bring them into the midst of this city; ⁵ and I Myself will battle against you with an outstretched mighty arm, with anger and rage and wrath. ⁶ I will strike the inhabitants of this city, man and beast: they shall die by a terrible pestilence. ⁷ And then—declares the LORD—I will deliver King Zedekiah of Judah and his courtiers and the people—those in this city who are left of the pestilence, of the sword, and of the famine—into the hands of King Nebuchadrezzar of Babylon, into the hands of their enemies, into the hands of those who seek their lives. He will put them to the sword without pity, without compassion, without mercy.

⁸ "And to this people you shall say: Thus said the LORD: I set before you the way of life and the way of death. ⁹ Whoever remains in this city shall die by the sword, by famine, and by pestilence; but whoever leaves and goes over to the Chaldeans who are besieging you shall live; ᵃ⁻he shall at least gain his life.⁻ᵃ ¹⁰ For I have set My face against this city for evil and not for good—declares the LORD. It shall be delivered into the hands of the king of Babylon, who will destroy it by fire."

¹¹ To the House of the king of Judah: Hear the word of the LORD! ¹² O House of David, thus said the LORD:

Render just verdicts
Morning by morning;
Rescue him who is robbed
From him who defrauded him.
Else My wrath will break forth like fire
And burn, with none to quench it,
Because of your wicked acts.

¹³ I will deal with you, ᵇ⁻O inhabitants of the valley,
O rock of the plain⁻ᵇ—declares the LORD—
You who say, "Who can come down against us?
Who can get into our lairs?"

¹⁴ I will punish you according to your deeds
—declares the LORD.

I will set fire to its forest;ᶜ
It shall consume all that is around it.

22

¹ Thus said the LORD: Go down to the palace of the king of Judah, where you shall utter this word. ² Say: Hear the word of the LORD: O king of Judah, you who sit on the throne of David, and your courtiers and your subjects who enter these gates! ³ Thus said the LORD: Do what is just and right; rescue from the defrauder him who is robbed; do not wrong the stranger, the fatherless, and the widow; commit no lawless act, and do not shed the blood of the innocent in this place. ⁴ For if you fulfill this command, then through the gates of this palace shall enter kings of David's line who sit upon his throne, riding horse-drawn chariots, with their courtiers and their subjects. ⁵ But if you do not heed these commands, I swear by Myself—declares the LORD—that this palace shall become a ruin.

⁶ For thus said the LORD concerning the royal palace of Judah:

You are as Gilead to Me,
As the summit of Lebanon;
But I will make you a desert,
Uninhabited towns.

⁷ I will appoint destroyers against you,

ᵃ⁻ᵃ Lit. "he shall have his life as booty"
ᵇ⁻ᵇ Force of Heb uncertain
ᶜ Perhaps a reference to the royal palace; cf. I Kings 7.2

JEREMIAH 22.8

Each with his tools;
They shall cut down your choicest cedars
And make them fall into the fire.

⁸ And when many nations pass by this city and one man asks another, "Why did the LORD do thus to that great city?" ⁹ the reply will be, "Because they forsook the covenant with the LORD their God and bowed down to other gods and served them."

¹⁰ Do not weep for the dead*ᵃ*
And do not lament for him;
Weep rather for *ᵇ*him who is leaving,*ᵇ*
For he shall never come back
To see the land of his birth!

¹¹ For thus said the LORD concerning Shallum*ᵇ* son of King Josiah of Judah, who succeeded his father Josiah as king, but who has gone forth from this place: He shall never come back. ¹² He shall die in the place to which he was exiled, and he shall not see this land again.

¹³ Ha! he who builds his house with unfairness
And his upper chambers with injustice,
Who makes his fellowman work without pay
And does not give him his wages,
¹⁴ Who thinks: I will build me a vast palace
With spacious upper chambers,
Provided with windows,
Paneled in cedar,
Painted with vermilion!
¹⁵ Do you think you are more a king
Because you compete in cedar?
Your father *ᶜ*ate and drank*ᶜ*
And dispensed justice and equity—
Then all went well with him.
¹⁶ He upheld the rights of the poor and needy—
Then all was well.
*ᵈ*That is truly heeding Me*ᵈ*
—declares the LORD.

¹⁷ But your eyes and your mind are only
On ill-gotten gains,
On shedding the blood of the innocent,
On committing fraud and violence.

¹⁸ Assuredly, thus said the LORD concerning Jehoiakim son of Josiah, king of Judah:
*ᵉ*They shall not mourn for him,
"Ah, brother! Ah, sister!"
They shall not mourn for him,
"Ah, lord! Ah, his majesty!"*ᵉ*
¹⁹ He shall have the burial of an ass,
Dragged out and left lying
Outside the gates of Jerusalem.

²⁰ Climb Lebanon and cry out,
Raise your voice in Bashan,
Cry out from Abarim,
For all your lovers are crushed.
²¹ I spoke to you when you were prosperous;
You said, "I will not listen."
That was your way ever since your youth,
You would not heed Me.
²² All your shepherds*ᶠ* shall be devoured by the wind,
And your lovers shall go into captivity.
Then you shall be shamed and humiliated
Because of all your depravity.
²³ You who dwell in Lebanon,
Nestled among the cedars,
*ᵍ*How much grace will you have*ᵍ*
When pains come upon you,
Travail as in childbirth!

²⁴ As I live—declares the LORD—*ʰ*if you, O Coniah, son of Jehoiakim, king of Judah, were*ʰ* a signet on my right hand, I would tear you off even from there. ²⁵ I will deliver you into the hands of those who seek your life, into the hands of those you dread, into the hands of King Nebuchadrezzar of Babylon and into the hands of the Chaldeans. ²⁶ I will hurl you and the mother who bore you into another land, where you were not born; there you shall both die. ²⁷ They shall not return to the land which they yearn to come back to.

---

*ᵃ*I.e. Josiah; see II Kings 23.29–30
*ᵇ⁻ᵇ*I.e. the king called by his throne name Jehoahaz in II Kings 23.31 ff., and by his private name Shallum here in v. 11 and in I Chron. 3.15
*ᶜ⁻ᶜ*I.e. he was content with the simple necessities of life
*ᵈ⁻ᵈ*Or "That is the reward for heeding Me"
*ᵉ⁻ᵉ*They shall express neither sorrow at the loss of a relative nor grief at the death of a ruler
*ᶠ*Change of vocalization yields "paramours"
*ᵍ⁻ᵍ*Septuagint reads "How you will groan"
*ʰ⁻ʰ*Heb "If Coniah . . . were . . ."; Coniah (Jeconiah in 24.1) is identical with Jehoiachin, II Kings 24.8 ff.

JEREMIAH 22·28

²⁸ Is this man Coniah
    A wretched broken pot,
    A vessel no one wants?
    Why are he and his offspring hurled out,
    And cast away in a land they knew not?
²⁹ O land, land, land,
    Hear the word of the Lord!
³⁰ Thus said the Lord:
    Record this man as without succession,
    One who shall never be found acceptable;
    For no man of his offspring shall be accepted
    To sit on the throne of David
    And to rule again in Judah.

23

¹ Ah, shepherds who let the flock of My pasture stray and scatter!—declares the Lord. ² Assuredly, thus said the Lord, the God of Israel, concerning the shepherds who should tend My people: It is you who let My flock scatter and go astray. You gave no thought to them, but I am going to give thought to you, for your wicked acts—declares the Lord. ³ And I Myself will gather the remnant of My flock from all the lands to which I have banished them, and I will bring them back to their pasture, where they shall be fertile and increase. ⁴ And I will appoint over them shepherds who will tend them; they shall no longer fear or be dismayed, and none of them shall be missing—declares the Lord.

⁵ See, the days are coming—declares the Lord—when I will raise up a true branch of David's line. He shall reign as king and shall prosper, and he shall do what is just and right in the land. ⁶ In his days Judah shall be delivered and Israel shall dwell secure. And this is the name by which he shall be called: "The Lord is our Vindicator."

⁷ Assuredly, days are coming—declares the Lord—when it shall no more be said, "As the Lord lives, who brought the Israelites out of the land of Egypt," ⁸ but rather, "As the Lord lives, who brought out and led the offspring of the House of Israel from the northland and from all the lands to which I have banished them." And they shall dwell upon their own soil.

⁹ Concerning the prophets.

    My heart is crushed within me,
    All my bones are trembling;^a
    I have become like a drunken man,
    Like one overcome by wine—
    Because of the Lord and His holy word.
¹⁰ For the land is full of adulterers,
    The land mourns because of ^{b-}a curse;^{-b}
    The pastures of the wilderness are dried up.
    ^{c-}For they run to do evil,
    They strain to do wrong.^{-c}
¹¹ For both prophet and priest are godless;
    Even in My House I find their wickedness
              —declares the Lord.
¹² Assuredly,
    Their path shall become
    Like slippery ground;
    They shall be thrust into darkness
    And there they shall fall;
    For I will bring disaster upon them,
    The year of their doom
              —declares the Lord.
¹³ In the prophets of Samaria
    I saw a repulsive thing:
    They prophesied by Baal
    And led My people Israel astray.
¹⁴ And in the prophets of Jerusalem
    I have seen a horrifying thing:
    Adultery and false dealing.
    They encourage evildoers,
    So that no one turns back from his wickedness.
    To Me they are all like Sodom,
    And its inhabitants like Gomorrah.
¹⁵ Assuredly, thus said the Lord of Hosts concerning the prophets:

    I am going to make them eat wormwood
    And drink a bitter draft;

---

^aMeaning of Heb uncertain
^{b-b}A few Heb mss. and Septuagint read "these"
^{c-c}Lit. "Their running is wickedness, / Their straining is iniquity"

JEREMIAH 23·16

For from the prophets of Jerusalem
Godlessness has gone forth to the whole land.

¹⁶ Thus said the LORD of Hosts:
Do not listen to the words of the prophets
Who prophesy to you;
They are deluding you:
The prophecies they speak are from their own minds,
Not from the mouth of the LORD.
¹⁷ They declare ᵈ⁻"the word of the LORD"
To men who despise Me:⁻ᵈ
"All shall be well with you";
And to all who follow their willful hearts they say:
"No evil shall befall you."
¹⁸ But he who has stood in the council of the LORD,
And seen, and heard His word—
He who has listened to His word must obey.ᵉ
¹⁹ ᶠ⁻Lo, the storm of the LORD goes forth in fury,
A whirling storm,
It shall whirl about the heads of the wicked.
²⁰ The anger of the LORD will not turn back
Till it has fulfilled and completed His purposes.⁻ᶠ
In the days to come
You shall clearly perceive it.

²¹ I did not send those prophets,
But they rushed in;
I did not speak to them,
Yet they prophesied.
²² If they have stood in My council,
Let them announce My words to My people
And make them turn back
From their evil ways and wicked acts.

²³ Am I only a God near at hand
        —says the LORD—
And not a God far away?
²⁴ If a man enters a hiding place,
Do I not see him
        —says the LORD.
For I fill both heaven and earth
        —declares the LORD.

²⁵ I have heard what the prophets say, who prophesy falsely in My name: "I had a dream, I had a dream." ²⁶ ᵃ⁻How long will there be⁻ᵃ in the minds of the prophets who prophesy falsehood—the prophets of their own deceitful minds— ²⁷ the plan to make My people forget My name, by means of the dreams which they tell each other, just as their fathers forgot My name because of Baal? ²⁸ Let the prophet who has a dream tell the dream; and let him who has received My word report My word faithfully! How can straw be compared to grain?—says the LORD. ²⁹ Behold, My word is like fire—declares the LORD—and like a hammer that shatters rock!

³⁰ Assuredly, I am going to deal with the prophets—declares the LORD—who steal My words from one another. ³¹ I am going to deal with the prophets—declares the LORD—who wagᵃ their tongues and make oracular utterances. ³² I am going to deal with those who prophesy lying dreams—declares the LORD—who relate them to lead My people astray with their reckless lies, when I did not send them or command them. They do this people no good—declares the LORD.

³³ And when this people—or a prophet or a priest—asks you, "What is the burdenᵍ of the LORD?" you shall answer them, ʰ⁻What is the burden?⁻ʰ I will cast you off—declares the LORD. ³⁴ As for the prophet or priest or layman who shall say "the burden of the LORD," I will punish that person and his house. ³⁵ Thus you shall speak to each other, every one to his fellow, "What has the LORD answered?" or "What has the LORD spoken?" ³⁶ But do not mention "the burden of the LORD" any more. ᵃ⁻Does a man regard his own word as a "burden,"⁻ᵃ that you pervert the words of the living God, the LORD of Hosts, our God? ³⁷ Thus you shall speak to the prophet, "What did the LORD answer you?" or "What did the LORD speak?" ³⁸ But if you say "the burden of the LORD"—assuredly, thus said the LORD: Because you said this thing, "the burden of the LORD," whereas I sent

---

ᵃ⁻ᵃ Meaning of Heb uncertain
ᵈ⁻ᵈ Septuagint reads "to men who despise the word of the LORD"
ᵉ Change of vocalization yields "announce it"; cf. vv. 22, 28
ᶠ⁻ᶠ This section constitutes the word of God to which Jeremiah refers
ᵍ I.e. pronouncement; cf. Isa. 13.1, where the word rendered "pronouncement" can also mean "burden"
ʰ⁻ʰ Septuagint and other versions read "You are the burden!"

JEREMIAH 23·39

word to you not to say "the burden of the Lord," ³⁹ I will utterly ⁱ⁻ⁱforget youⁱ and I will cast you away from My presence, together with the city which I gave to you and your fathers. ⁴⁰ And I will lay upon you a disgrace for all time, shame for all time, which shall never be forgotten.

24

¹ The Lord showed me two baskets of figs, placed in front of the Temple of the Lord. This was after King Nebuchadrezzar of Babylon had exiled King Jeconiah son of Jehoiakim of Judah, and the officials of Judah, and the craftsmen and smiths, from Jerusalem, and had brought them to Babylon. ² One basket contained very good figs, like first-ripened figs, and the other basket contained very bad figs, so bad that they could not be eaten.
³ And the Lord said to me, "What do you see, Jeremiah?" I answered, "Figs—the good ones are very good, and the bad ones very bad, so bad that they cannot be eaten."
⁴ Then the word of the Lord came to me:
⁵ Thus said the Lord, the God of Israel: As with these good figs, so will I single out for good the Judean exiles whom I have driven out from this place to the land of the Chaldeans. ⁶ I will look upon them favorably, and I will bring them back to this land; I will build them and not overthrow them; I will plant them and not uproot them. ⁷ And I will give them the understanding to acknowledge Me, for I am the Lord. And they shall be My people and I will be their God, when they turn back to Me with all their heart.
⁸ And like the bad figs, which are so bad that they cannot be eaten—thus said the Lord—so will I treat King Zedekiah of Judah and his officials and the remnant of Jerusalem that is left in this land, and those who are living in the land of Egypt: ⁹ I will make them a horror—an evil—to all the kingdoms of the earth, a disgrace and a proverb, a byword and a curseᵃ in all the places to which I banish them. ¹⁰ I will send the sword, famine, and pestilence against them until they are exterminated from the land which I gave to them and their fathers.

25

¹ The word which came to Jeremiah concerning all the people of Judah, in the fourth year of King Jehoiakim son of Josiah of Judah, which was the first year of King Nebuchadrezzar of Babylon. ² This is what the prophet Jeremiah said to all the people of Judah and to all the inhabitants of Jerusalem:

³ From the thirteenth year of King Josiah son of Amon of Judah, to this day—these twenty-three years—the word of the Lord has come to me. I have spoken to you persistently, but you would not listen. ⁴ Moreover, the Lord constantly sent all his servants the prophets to you, but you would not listen or incline your ears to hear ⁵ when they said, "Turn back, everyone, from your evil ways and your wicked acts, that you may remain throughout the ages on the soil which the Lord gave to you and your fathers. ⁶ Do not follow other gods, to serve them and worship them. Do not vex Me with what your own hands have made,ᵃ and I will not bring disaster upon you." ⁷ But you would not listen to Me—declares the Lord—but vexed Me with what your hands made, to your own hurt.
⁸ Assuredly, thus said the Lord of Hosts: Because you would not listen to My words, ⁹ I am going to send for all the peoples of the north—declares the Lord—and for My servant, King Nebuchadrezzar of Babylon, and bring them against this land and its inhabitants, and against all those nations round about. I will exterminate them and make them a desolation, an object of hissingᵇ—ruins for all time. ¹⁰ And I will banish from them the sound of mirth and gladness, the voice of bridegroom and bride, and the sound of the mill and the light of the lamp. ¹¹ This whole land shall be a desolate ruin.

ⁱ⁻ⁱSome Heb mss., Septuagint, and other versions read "lift you up," a word from the same root as "burden"

ᵃI.e. a standard by which men curse; cf. Gen. 12.2; Zech. 8.13

ᵃI.e. idols
ᵇCf. note at 18.6

JEREMIAH 25·12

And those nations shall serve the king of Babylon seventy years. ¹² When the seventy years are over, I will punish the king of Babylon and that nation and the land of the Chaldeans for their sins—declares the LORD—and I will make it a desolation for all time. ¹³ And I will bring upon that land all that I have decreed against it, all that is recorded in this book—that which Jeremiah prophesied against all the nations. ¹⁴ For they too shall be enslaved by many nations and great kings; and I will requite them according to their acts and according to their conduct.

¹⁵ For thus said the LORD, the God of Israel, to me: "Take from My hand this cup of wine—of wrath—and make all the nations to whom I send you drink of it. ¹⁶ Let them drink and retch and act crazy, because of the sword which I am sending among them."

¹⁷ So I took the cup from the hand of the LORD and gave drink to all the nations to whom the LORD had sent me: ¹⁸ Jerusalem and the towns of Judah, and its kings and officials, to make them a desolate ruin, an object of hissing and a curse^c—as is now the case; ¹⁹ Pharaoh king of Egypt, his courtiers, his officials, and all his people; ²⁰ all ^{d-}the mixed peoples;^{-d} all the kings of the land of Uz; all the kings of the land of the Philistines—Ashkelon, Gaza, Ekron, and what is left of Ashdod; ²¹ Edom, Moab and Ammon; ²² all the kings of Tyre and all the kings of Sidon, and all the kings of the coastland across the sea; ²³ Dedan, Tema, and Buz, and all those who have their hair clipped; ²⁴ all the kings of Arabia, and all the kings of ^{d-}the mixed peoples^{-d} who live in the desert; ²⁵ all the kings of Zimri^d and all the kings of Elam and all the kings of Media; ²⁶ all the kings of the north, whether far from or close to each other—all the ^{d-}royal lands which are on the earth.^{-d} And last of all, the king of Sheshach^e shall drink.

²⁷ Say to them: "Thus said the LORD of Hosts, the God of Israel: Drink and get drunk and vomit; fall and never rise again, because of the sword that I send among you." ²⁸ And if they refuse to take the cup from your hand and drink, say to them, "Thus said the LORD of Hosts: You must drink! ²⁹ If I am bringing the punishment first on the city that bears My name, do you expect to go unpunished? You will not go unpunished, for I am summoning the sword against all the inhabitants of the earth—declares the LORD."

³⁰ You are to prophesy all those things to them, and then say to them:

> The LORD roars from on high,
> He makes His voice heard from His holy dwelling;
> He roars aloud over His [earthly] abode;
> He utters shouts like the grape-treaders,
> Against all the dwellers on earth.
> ³¹ Tumult has reached the ends of the earth,
> For the LORD has a case against the nations,
> He contends with all flesh.
> He delivers the wicked to the sword
>   —declares the LORD.

³² Thus said the LORD of Hosts:
> Disaster goes forth
> From nation to nation;
> A great storm is unleashed
> From the remotest parts of earth.

³³ In that day, the earth shall be strewn with the slain of the LORD from one end to the other. They shall not be mourned, or gathered and buried; they shall become dung upon the face of the earth.

³⁴ Howl, you shepherds, and yell,
> Strew [dust] on yourselves, you lords of the flock!
> For the day of your slaughter draws near.
> ^{d-}I will break you in pieces,^{-d}
> And you shall fall like a precious vessel.
> ³⁵ Flight shall fail the shepherds,
> And escape, the lords of the flock.
> ³⁶ Hark, the outcry of the shepherds,
> And the howls of the lords of the flock!
> For the LORD is ravaging their pasture.
> ³⁷ The peaceful meadows shall be wiped out
> By the fierce wrath of the LORD.
> ³⁸ Like a lion, He has gone forth from His lair;
> The land has become a desolation,
> Because of the oppressive wrath,
> Because of His fierce anger.

^cCf. note at 24.9   ^{d-d}Meaning of Heb uncertain
^eA cipher for *Babel*, Babylon

26

¹ At the beginning of the reign of King Jehoiakim son of Josiah of Judah, this word came from the LORD:
² "Thus said the LORD: Stand in the court of the House of the LORD, and speak to [the men of] all the towns of Judah, who are coming to worship in the House of the LORD, all the words which I command you to speak to them. Do not omit anything. ³ Perhaps they will listen and turn back, each from his evil way, that I may renounce the punishment I am planning to bring upon them for their wicked acts. ⁴ And say to them:

"Thus said the LORD: If you do not obey Me, abiding by the Teaching which I have set before you, ⁵ heeding the words of My servants the prophets whom I have been sending to you persistently—but you have not heeded— ⁶ then I will make this House like Shiloh, and I will make this city a curse[a] for all the nations of earth."

⁷ The priests and prophets and all the people heard Jeremiah speaking these words in the House of the LORD. ⁸ And when Jeremiah finished speaking all that the LORD had commanded him to speak to all the people, they seized him—priests and prophets and all the people—saying, "You shall die! ⁹ How dare you prophesy in the name of the LORD that this House shall become like Shiloh and this city be made desolate, without inhabitants?" And all the people crowded about Jeremiah in the House of the LORD.

¹⁰ When the officials of Judah heard about this, they went up from the king's palace to the House of the LORD and held a session at the entrance of the New Gate of [b-]the House of[-b] the LORD. ¹¹ The priests and prophets said to the officials and to all the people, "This man deserves the death penalty, for he has prophesied against this city, as you yourselves have heard."

¹² Jeremiah said to the officials and to all the people, "It was the LORD who sent me to prophesy against this House and this city all the words you heard. ¹³ Therefore mend your ways and your acts, and heed the LORD your God, that the LORD may renounce the punishment He has decreed for you. ¹⁴ As for me, I am in your hands: do to me what seems good and right to you. ¹⁵ But know that if you put me to death, you will be putting the blood of an innocent man upon yourselves, and upon this city and its inhabitants; for in truth the LORD has sent me to you, to speak all these words to you."

¹⁶ Then the officials and all the people said to the priests and prophets, "This man does not deserve the death penalty, for he spoke to us in the name of the LORD our God."

¹⁷ And some of the elders of the land arose and said to the entire assemblage of the people, ¹⁸ "Micah the Morashtite, who prophesied in the days of King Hezekiah of Judah, said to all the people of Judah: 'Thus said the LORD of Hosts:

Zion shall be plowed as a field,
Jerusalem shall become heaps of ruins,
And the Temple Mount a shrine in the woods.'[c]

¹⁹ Did King Hezekiah of Judah, and all Judah, put him to death? Did he not rather fear the LORD and implore the LORD, so that the LORD renounced the punishment He had decreed against them? We are about to do great injury to ourselves!"

²⁰ There was also a man prophesying in the name of the LORD, Uriah son of Shemaiah from Kiriath-jearim, who prophesied against this city and this land the same things as Jeremiah. ²¹ King Jehoiakim and all his warriors and all the officials heard about his address, and the king wanted to put him to death. Uriah heard of this and fled in fear, and came to Egypt. ²² But King Jehoiakim sent men to Egypt, Elnathan son of Achbor and men with him to Egypt. ²³ They took Uriah out of Egypt and brought him to King Jehoiakim, who had him put to the sword and his body thrown into the burial place of the common people. ²⁴ However, Ahikam son of Shaphan protected Jeremiah, so that he was not handed over to the people for execution.

---

[a] Cf. note at 24.9
[b-b] So many mss. and ancient versions; other mss. and editions omit these words
[c] Mic. 3.12

27

¹ At the beginning of the reign of King Jehoiakim[a] son of Josiah of Judah, this word came to Jeremiah from the LORD:

² Thus said the LORD to me: Make for yourself thongs and bars of a yoke, and put them on your neck. ³ [b-And send them-b] to the king of Edom, the king of Moab, the king of the Ammonites, the king of Tyre, and the king of Sidon, by envoys who have come to Jerusalem, to King Zedekiah of Judah; ⁴ and give them this charge to their masters: Thus said the LORD of Hosts, the God of Israel: Say this to your masters:
⁵ It is I who made the earth, and the men and beasts who are on the earth, by My great might and My outstretched arm; and I give it to whomever I deem proper. ⁶ I herewith deliver all these lands to My servant, King Nebuchadnezzar of Babylon; I even give him the wild beasts to serve him. ⁷ All nations shall serve him, his son and his grandson—until the turn of his own land comes, when many nations and great kings shall subjugate him. ⁸ The nation or kingdom that does not serve him—King Nebuchadnezzar of Babylon—and does not put its neck under the yoke of the king of Babylon, that nation I will visit—declares the LORD—with sword, famine, and pestilence, until I have destroyed it by his hands. ⁹ As for you, give no heed to your prophets, augurs, dreamers,[c] diviners, and sorcerers, who say to you, "Do not serve the king of Babylon." ¹⁰ For they prophesy falsely to you—with the result that you shall be banished from your land; I will drive you out and you shall perish. ¹¹ But the nation which puts its neck under the yoke of the king of Babylon, and serves him, will be left by Me on its own soil—declares the LORD—to till it and dwell on it.
¹² I also spoke to King Zedekiah of Judah in just the same way: "Put your necks under the yoke of the king of Babylon; serve him and his people, and live! ¹³ Otherwise you will die together with your people, by sword, famine, and pestilence, as the LORD has decreed against any nation that does not serve the king of Babylon. ¹⁴ Give no heed to the words of the prophets who say to you, 'Do not serve the king of Babylon,' for they prophesy falsely to you. ¹⁵ I have not sent them—declares the LORD—and they prophesy falsely in My name, with the result that I will drive you out and you shall perish, together with the prophets who prophesy to you."
¹⁶ And to the priests and to all that people I said: "Thus said the LORD: Give no heed to the words of the prophets who prophesy to you, 'The vessels of the House of the LORD shall shortly be brought back from Babylon,' for they prophesy falsely to you. ¹⁷ Give them no heed. Serve the king of Babylon, and live! Otherwise this city shall become a ruin. ¹⁸ If they are really prophets and the word of the LORD is with them, let them intercede with the LORD of Hosts not to let the vessels remaining in the House of the LORD, in the royal palace of Judah, and in Jerusalem, go to Babylon!
¹⁹ "For thus said the LORD of Hosts concerning the columns, the tank,[d] the stands, and the rest of the vessels remaining in this city, ²⁰ which King Nebuchadnezzar of Babylon did not take when he exiled King Jeconiah son of Jehoiakim of Judah, from Jerusalem to Babylon, with all the nobles of Judah and Jerusalem; ²¹ for thus said the LORD of Hosts, the God of Israel, concerning the vessels remaining in the House of the LORD, in the royal palace of Judah, and in Jerusalem: ²² They shall be brought to Babylon, and there they shall remain, until I take note of them—declares the LORD of Hosts—and bring them up and restore them to this place."

28

¹ That year, early in the reign of King Zedekiah of Judah, in the fifth month of the fourth year, the prophet Hananiah son of Azzur, who was from Gibeon, spoke to me in the House of the LORD, in the presence of the priests and all the people. He

---

[a] Emendation yields "Zedekiah"; so a few mss. and Syriac; cf. vv. 3 and 12
[b-b] Emendation yields "And send," i.e. a message
[c] Lit. "dreams"
[d] Lit. "sea"; cf. I Kings 7.23 ff.

JEREMIAH 28.2

said: ² "Thus said the LORD of Hosts, the God of Israel: I hereby break the yoke of the king of Babylon. ³ In two years, I will restore to this place all the vessels of the House of the LORD which King Nebuchadnezzar of Babylon took from this place and brought to Babylon. ⁴ And I will bring back to this place King Jeconiah son of Jehoiakim of Judah, and all the Judean exiles who went to Babylon—declares the LORD. Yes, I will break the yoke of the king of Babylon."

⁵ Then the prophet Jeremiah answered the prophet Hananiah in the presence of the priests and of all the people who were standing in the House of the LORD. ⁶ The prophet Jeremiah said: "Amen! May the LORD do so! May the LORD fulfill what you have prophesied and bring back from Babylon to this place the vessels of the House of the LORD and all the exiles! ⁷ But just listen to this word which I address to you and to all the people: ⁸ The prophets who lived before you and me from ancient times prophesied war, disaster, and pestilence against many lands and great kingdoms. ⁹ So if a prophet prophesies good fortune, then only when the word of the prophet comes true can it be known that the LORD really sent him."

¹⁰ But the prophet Hananiah removed the bar from the neck of the prophet Jeremiah, and broke it; ¹¹ and Hananiah said in the presence of all the people, "Thus said the LORD: So will I break the yoke of King Nebuchadnezzar of Babylon from off the necks of the nations, in two years." And the prophet Jeremiah went on his way.

¹² After the prophet Hananiah had broken the bar from off the neck of the prophet Jeremiah, the word of the LORD came to Jeremiah: ¹³ "Go say to Hananiah: Thus said the LORD: You broke bars of wood, but ᵃ⁻you shall⁻ᵃ make bars of iron instead. ¹⁴ For thus said the LORD of Hosts, the God of Israel: I have put an iron yoke upon the necks of all those nations, that they may serve King Nebuchadnezzar of Babylon—and serve him they shall! I have even given the wild beasts to him."

¹⁵ And the prophet Jeremiah said to the prophet Hananiah, "Listen, Hananiah! The LORD did not send you, and you have given this people lying assurances. ¹⁶ Assuredly, thus said the LORD: I am going to banish you from off the earth. This year you shall die, for you have urged disloyalty to the LORD."

¹⁷ And the prophet Hananiah died that year, in the seventh month.

29

¹ This is the text of the letter which the prophet Jeremiah sent from Jerusalem to the priests, the prophets, the rest of the elders of the exile community, and to all the people whom Nebuchad-

ᵃ⁻ᵃ Septuagint reads "I will"

JEREMIAH 29·2

nezzar had exiled from Jerusalem to Babylon— ² after King Jeconiah, the queen mother, the eunuchs, the officials of Judah and Jerusalem, and the craftsmen and smiths had left Jerusalem. ³ [The letter was sent] through Elasah son of Shaphan and Gemariah son of Hilkiah, whom King Zedekiah of Judah had dispatched to Babylon, to King Nebuchadnezzar of Babylon.

⁴ Thus said the LORD of Hosts, the God of Israel, to the whole community which I exiled from Jerusalem to Babylon: ⁵ Build houses and live in them, plant gardens and eat their fruit. ⁶ Take wives and beget sons and daughters; and take wives for your sons, and give your daughters to husbands, that they may bear sons and daughters. Multiply there, do not decrease. ⁷ And seek the welfare of the city to which I have exiled you and pray to the LORD in its behalf; for in its prosperity you shall prosper.
⁸ For thus said the LORD of Hosts, the God of Israel: Let not the prophets and diviners in your midst deceive you, and pay no heed to the dreams they[a] dream. ⁹ For they prophesy to you in My name falsely; I did not send them—declares the LORD.
¹⁰ For thus said the LORD: When Babylon's seventy years are over, I will take note of you, and I will fulfill to you My promise of favor—to bring you back to this place. ¹¹ For I am mindful of the plans I have made concerning you—declares the LORD—plans for your welfare, not for disaster, to give you a hopeful future. ¹² When you call Me, and come and pray to Me, I will give heed to you. ¹³ You will search for Me and find Me, if only you seek Me with all your hearts. ¹⁴ I will be at hand for you—declares the LORD—and I will restore your fortunes. And I will gather you from all the nations and from all the places to which I have banished you—declares the LORD—and I will bring you back to the place from which I have exiled you.
¹⁵ But you say, the LORD has raised up prophets for us in Babylon.[b]

¹⁶ Thus said the LORD concerning the king who sits on the throne of David, and concerning all the people who dwell in this city, your brothers who did not go out with you into exile— ¹⁷ thus said the LORD of Hosts: I am going to let loose sword, famine, pestilence against them and I will treat them as loathsome figs, so bad that they cannot be eaten.[c] ¹⁸ I will pursue them with the sword, with famine, and with pestilence; and I will make them a horror to all the kingdoms of the earth, a curse and an object of horror and hissing[d] and scorn among all the nations to which I shall banish them, ¹⁹ because they did not heed My words—declares the LORD—when I persistently sent to them My servants, the prophets, and they[a] did not heed—declares the LORD.

²⁰ But you, the whole exile community which I banished from Jerusalem to Babylon, ²¹ hear the word of the LORD! Thus said the LORD of Hosts, the God of Israel, concerning Ahab son of Kolaiah and Zedekiah son of Maaseiah, who prophesy falsely to you in My name: I am going to deliver them into the hands of King Nebuchadrezzar of Babylon, and he shall put them to death before your eyes. ²² And the whole exile community of Judah shall use a curse derived from their fate: "May God make you like Zedekiah and Ahab, whom the king of Babylon consigned to the flames!"— ²³ because they did vile things in Israel, committing adultery with the wives of their fellows and speaking in My name false words which I had not commanded them. I am He who knows and bears witness—declares the LORD.
²⁴ Concerning Shemaiah the Nehelamite you[e] shall say: ²⁵ Thus said the LORD of Hosts, the God of Israel: Because you sent letters in your own name to all the people in Jerusalem, to Zephaniah son of Maaseiah the priest and to the rest of the priests, as follows, ²⁶ "The LORD appointed you priest in place of the priest Jehoiada, so that there might be authority[f] in the House of the LORD over every

---

[a] Heb "you"
[b] This v. is continued in vv. 20 ff.
[c] Cf. 24.1 ff.
[d] Cf. note at 18.16
[e] I.e. Jeremiah
[f] Lit. "officials"

JEREMIAH 29·27

madman who wants to play the prophet, to put him into the cell *g-*and into the stocks.*-g* ²⁷ Now why have you not rebuked Jeremiah the Anathothite, who plays the prophet among you? ²⁸ For he has actually sent a message to us in Babylon to this effect: It will be a long time. Build houses and live in them, plant gardens and enjoy their fruit."—

²⁹ When the priest Zephaniah read this letter in the hearing of the prophet Jeremiah, ³⁰ the word of the LORD came to Jeremiah: ³¹ Send a message to the entire exile community: Thus said the LORD concerning Shemaiah the Nehelamite: Because Shemaiah prophesied to you, though I did not send him, and made you false promises, ³² assuredly, thus said the LORD: I am going to deal with Shemaiah the Nehelamite and his offspring. There shall be no man of his line dwelling among this people or seeing the good things I am going to do for My people—declares the LORD—for he has urged disloyalty toward the LORD.

30

¹ The word which came to Jeremiah from the LORD: ² Thus said the LORD, the God of Israel: Write down in a scroll all the words that I have spoken to you. ³ For days are coming—declares the LORD—when I will restore the fortunes of My people Israel and Judah, said the LORD; and I will bring them back to the land which I gave their fathers, and they shall possess it. ⁴ And these are the words which the LORD spoke concerning Israel and Judah:

⁵ Thus said the LORD:

We have heard cries of panic,
Terror without relief.
⁶ Ask and see:
Surely males do not bear young!
Why then do I see every man
With his hands on his loins
Like a woman in labor?
Why have all faces turned pale?
⁷ Ah, that day is awesome;
There is none like it!
It is a time of trouble for Jacob,
But he shall be delivered from it.

⁸ In that day—declares the LORD of Hosts—I will break the yoke from off your neck and I will rip off your bonds. Strangers shall no longer make slaves of them; ⁹ instead, they shall serve the LORD their God and David, the king whom I will raise up for them.

¹⁰ But you,
Have no fear, My servant Jacob
—declares the LORD—
Be not dismayed, O Israel!
I will deliver you from far away,
Your folk from their land of captivity.
And Jacob shall again have calm
And quiet with none to trouble him;
¹¹ For I am with you to deliver you
—declares the LORD.
I will make an end of all the nations
Among which I have dispersed you;
But I will not make an end of you!
I will not leave you unpunished,
But I will chastise you in measure.

¹² For thus said the LORD:

Your injury is incurable,
Your wound severe;
¹³ *a-*No one pleads for the healing of your sickness,*-a*
There is no recovery for you.
¹⁴ All your friends have forgotten you,
They do not seek you out;
For I have struck you as an enemy strikes,
With cruel chastisement,
Because your iniquity was so great
And your sins so many.
¹⁵ Why cry out over your injury,
That your wound is incurable?
I did these things to you

---

*g-g*Meaning of Heb uncertain

*a-a*Meaning of Heb uncertain

JEREMIAH 30·16

Because your iniquity was so great
And your sins so many.

16 Assuredly,
All who wanted to devour you shall be devoured,
And every one of your foes shall go into captivity;
All who despoiled you shall be despoiled,
And all who pillaged you I will give up to pillage.
17 But I will bring healing to you
And cure you of your wounds
—declares the LORD.

Though they called you "Outcast,
That Zion whom no one seeks out,"
18 Thus said the LORD:

I will restore the fortunes of Jacob's tents
And have compassion upon his dwellings.
The city shall be rebuilt on its mound,[b]
And the citadel in its proper place.
19 From them shall issue thanksgiving
And the sound of dancers.
I will multiply them,
And they shall not be few;
I will make them honored,
And they shall not be humbled.
20 His children shall be as of old,
And his community shall be established by My grace;
And I will deal with all his oppressors.
21 His chieftain shall be one of his own,
His ruler shall come from his midst;
I will bring him near, that he may approach Me
—declares the LORD—
For who would otherwise dare approach Me?
22 You shall be My people,
And I will be your God.

23 Lo, the storm of the LORD goes forth in fury,
A raging tempest;
It shall whirl down upon the head of the wicked.
24 The anger of the LORD shall not turn back
Till it has fulfilled and completed His purposes.
In the days to come
You shall perceive it.

[31] 1 [c]At that time—declares the LORD—I will be God to all the clans of Israel, and they shall be My people.

31

2 Thus said the LORD:
The people escaped from the sword,
Found favor in the wilderness;
When Israel was marching homeward,
3 The LORD revealed Himself to me[a] of old.
Eternal love I conceived for you then;
Therefore I continue My grace to you.
4 I will build you firmly again,
O Maiden Israel!
Again you shall take up your timbrels
And go forth to the rhythm of the dancers.
5 Again you shall plant vineyards
On the hills of Samaria;
Men shall plant and live to enjoy them.
6 For the day is coming when watchmen
Shall proclaim on the heights of Ephraim:
Come, let us go up to Zion,
To the LORD our God!

7 For thus said the LORD:

Cry out in joy for Jacob,
Shout at the crossroads[b] of the nations!
Sing aloud in praise, and say:
[c-]Save, O LORD, Your people,[-c]
The remnant of Israel.
8 I will bring them in from the northland,
Gather them from the ends of the earth—
The blind and the lame among them,
Those with child and those in labor—
In a vast throng they shall return here.
9 They shall come with weeping.
And graciously[d] will I guide them.
I will lead them to streams of water,

---

[b]I.e. on the mound of ruins left by its previous destruction
[c]In some editions, this verse is 30.25

[a]Emendation yields "him"
[b]Lit. "head"; cf. Ezek. 21.24
[c-c]Emendation yields "The LORD has saved His people"
[d]For this meaning, cf. Zech. 12.10

By a level road where they will not stumble.
For I am ever a Father to Israel,
Ephraim is My firstborn.

10 Hear the word of the LORD, O nations,
And tell it in the isles afar.
Say:
He who scattered Israel will gather them,
And will guard them as a shepherd his flock.
11 For the LORD will ransom Jacob,
Redeem him from one too strong for him.
12 They shall come and shout on the heights of Zion,
Radiant over the bounty of the LORD—
Over new grain and wine and oil,
And over sheep and cattle.
They shall fare like a watered garden,
They shall never languish again.
13 Then shall maidens dance gaily,
Young men and old alike.
I will turn their mourning to joy,
I will comfort them and cheer them in their grief.
14 I will give the priests their fill of fatness,
And My people shall enjoy My full bounty
—declares the LORD.

15 Thus said the LORD:
A cry is heard *-in Ramah-*—
Wailing, bitter weeping—
Rachel weeping for her children.
She refuses to be comforted
For her children, who are gone.
16 Thus said the LORD:
Restrain your voice from weeping,
Your eyes from shedding tears;
For there is a reward for your labor
—declares the LORD:
They shall return from the enemy's land.
17 And there is hope for your future
—declares the LORD:
Your children shall return to their country.

18 I can hear Ephraim lamenting:
You have chastised me, and I am chastised
Like a calf that has not been broken.
Receive me back, let me return,
For You, O LORD, are my God.
19 Now that I have turned back, I am filled with remorse;
Now that I am made aware, I strike my thigh.*
I am ashamed and humiliated,
For I bear the disgrace of my youth.
20 Truly, Ephraim is a dear son to Me,
A child that is dandled!
Whenever I have turned*g* against him,
My thoughts would dwell on him still.
That is why My heart yearns for him;
I will receive him back in love
—declares the LORD.
21 Set up signposts,
Erect markers;*h*
Keep in mind the highway,
The road that you traveled.
Return, Maiden Israel!
Return to these towns of yours!
22 How long will you waver,
O rebellious daughter?
(For the LORD has created something new on earth:
A woman courts*h* a man.)

23 Thus said the LORD of Hosts, the God of Israel: They shall again say this in the land of Judah and in its towns, when I restore their fortunes:
"The LORD bless you,
Abode of righteousness,
O holy mountain!"
24 Judah and all its towns alike shall be inhabited by the farmers and *i-*those who move about*-i* with the flocks. 25 For I will give the thirsty abundant drink, and satisfy all who languish.

26 At this I awoke and looked about, and my sleep*j* had been pleasant to me.

27 See, the days are coming—declares the LORD—when I will sow the House of Israel and the House of Judah with seed of men and seed of cattle; 28 and just as I was watchful over them to uproot and to pull down, to overthrow and to de-

---
*e-e*Or "on a height"
*f*I.e. as a gesture of self-reproach
*g*Lit. "spoken"
*h*Meaning of Heb uncertain
*i-i*Lit. "they shall travel"
*j*I.e. the vision in the preceding verses

JEREMIAH 31·29

stroy and to bring disaster, so I will be watchful over them to build and to plant—declares the Lord. ²⁹ In those days, they shall no longer say, "Fathers have eaten sour grapes and children's teeth are set on edge." ³⁰ But everyone shall die for his own sins: whosoever eats sour grapes, his teeth shall be set on edge.

³¹ See, days are coming—declares the Lord—when I will make a new covenant with the House of Israel and the House of Judah. ³² It will not be like the covenant I made with their fathers, when I took them by the hand to lead them out of the land of Egypt, a covenant which they broke, so that I rejected*ᵏ* them—declares the Lord. ³³ But such shall be the covenant I will make with the House of Israel after these days—declares the Lord: I will put My Teaching into their inmost being and inscribe it upon their hearts. Then I will be their God, and they shall be My people. ³⁴ No longer will they need to teach one another and say to one another, "Heed the Lord"; for all of them, from the least of them to the greatest, shall heed Me—declares the Lord.

> For I will forgive their iniquities,
> And remember their sins no more.

³⁵ Thus said the Lord,
> Who established the sun for light by day,
> The laws of moon and stars for light by night,
> Who stirs up the sea into roaring waves,
> Whose name is Lord of Hosts:

³⁶ If these laws should ever be annulled by Me
> —declares the Lord—
> Only then would the offspring of Israel cease
> To be a nation before Me for all time.

³⁷ Thus said the Lord: If the heavens above could be measured, and the foundations of the earth below could be fathomed, only then would I reject all the offspring of Israel for all that they have done—declares the Lord.

³⁸ See, days are coming—declares the Lord—when the city shall be rebuilt for the Lord from the Tower of Hananel to the Corner Gate; ³⁹ and the measuring line shall go straight out to the Gareb Hill, and then turn toward Goah. ⁴⁰ And the entire Valley of the Corpses and the Ashes, and all the fields as far as the wadi Kidron, and the corner of the Horse Gate on the east, shall be holy to the Lord. They shall never again be uprooted or overthrown.

32

¹ The word which came to Jeremiah from the Lord in the tenth year of King Zedekiah of Judah, which was the eighteenth year of Nebuchadrezzar. ² At that time the army of the king of Babylon was besieging Jerusalem, and the prophet Jeremiah was confined in the prison compound attached to the palace of the king of Judah. ³ For King Zedekiah of Judah had confined him, saying, "How dare you prophesy: 'Thus said the Lord: I am delivering this city into the hands of the king of Babylon, and he shall capture it. ⁴ And King Zedekiah of Judah shall not escape from the Chaldeans; he shall be delivered into the hands of the king of Babylon, *ᵃ*and he shall speak to him face to face and see him in person.*ᵃ* ⁵ And Zedekiah shall be brought to Babylon, there to remain until I take note of him—declares the Lord. When you wage war against the Chaldeans, you shall not be successful.'"

⁶ Jeremiah said: The word of the Lord came to me: ⁷ Hanamel, the son of your uncle Shallum, will come to you and say, "Buy my land in Anathoth, *ᵇ*for you are next in succession to redeem it by purchase."*ᵇ* ⁸ And just as the Lord had said, my cousin Hanamel came to me in the prison compound and said to me, "Please buy my land in Anathoth, in the territory of Benjamin; for the right of succession is yours, and you have the duty of redemption. Buy it." Then I knew that it was indeed the word of the Lord.

ᵏTaking *ba'alti* as equivalent to *bahalti*; cf. 3.14

ᵃ⁻ᵃLit. "and his mouth shall speak with his mouth, and his eyes shall see his eyes"
ᵇ⁻ᵇLit. "for yours is the procedure of redemption by purchase"

JEREMIAH 32·9

⁹ So I bought the land in Anathoth from my cousin Hanamel. I weighed out the money to him, seventeen shekels of silver. ¹⁰ I wrote a deed, sealed it, and had it witnessed; and I weighed out the silver on a balance. ¹¹ I took the deed of purchase, the sealed text and the open one ᶜ⁻according to rule and law,⁻ᶜ ¹² and gave the deed to Baruch son of Neriah son of Mahseiah in the presence of my kinsman Hanamel, of the witnesses ᵈ⁻who were named⁻ᵈ in the deed, and all the Judeans who were sitting in the prison compound. ¹³ In their presence I charged Baruch as follows: ¹⁴ Thus said the LORD of Hosts, the God of Israel: "Take these documents, this deed of purchase, the sealed text and the open one, and put them into an earthen jar, so that they may last a long time." ¹⁵ For thus said the LORD of Hosts, the God of Israel: "Houses, fields, and vineyards shall again be purchased in this land."

¹⁶ But after I had given the deed to Baruch son of Neriah, I prayed to the LORD: ¹⁷ "Ah, Lord GOD! You made heaven and earth with Your great might and outstretched arm. Nothing is too wondrous for You! ¹⁸ You show kindness to the thousandth generation, but visit the guilt of the fathers upon their children after them. O great and mighty God whose name is LORD of Hosts, ¹⁹ wondrous in purpose and mighty in deed, whose eyes observe all the ways of men, so as to repay every man according to his ways, and with the proper fruit of his deeds! ²⁰ You displayed signs and marvels in the land of Egypt ᵉ⁻with lasting effect,⁻ᵉ and won renown in Israel and among mankind to this very day. ²¹ You freed Your people Israel from the land of Egypt with signs and marvels, with a strong hand and an outstretched arm, and with great terror. ²² You gave them this land which You had sworn to their fathers to give them, a land flowing with milk and honey, ²³ and they came and took possession of it. But they did not listen to You or follow Your Teaching; they did nothing of what You commanded them to do. Therefore you have caused all this misfortune to befall them. ²⁴ Here are the siege-mounds, raised against the city to storm it; and the city, because of sword and famine and disease, is at the mercy of the Chaldeans who are attacking it. What You threatened has come to pass—as You see. ²⁵ Yet You, Lord GOD, said to me: Buy the land for money and call in witnesses—when the city is at the mercy of the Chaldeans!"

²⁶ Then the word of the LORD came to Jeremiah:

²⁷ "Behold I am the LORD, the God of all flesh. Is anything too wondrous for Me? ²⁸ Assuredly, thus said the LORD: I am delivering this city into the hands of the Chaldeans and of King Nebuchadrezzar of Babylon, and he shall capture it. ²⁹ And the Chaldeans who have been attacking this city shall come and set this city on fire and burn it down—with the houses on whose roofs they made offerings to Baal and poured out libations to other gods, so as to vex Me. ³⁰ For the people of Israel and Judah have done nothing but evil in My sight since their youth; they have done nothing but vex Me by their conduct—declares the LORD. ³¹ This city has aroused My anger and My wrath from the day it was built until this day; so that it must be removed from My sight ³² because of all the wickedness of the people of Israel and Judah who have so acted as to vex Me—they, their kings, their officials, their priests and prophets, and the men of Judah and the inhabitants of Jerusalem. ³³ They turned their backs to Me, not their faces; though I have taught them persistently, they do not give heed or accept rebuke. ³⁴ They placed their abominations in the House which bears My name and defiled it; ³⁵ and they built the shrines of Baal which are in the Valley of Ben-hinnom, where they offered up their sons and daughters to Molech—when I had never commanded, or even thought [of commanding], that they should do such an abominable thing, and so bring guilt on Judah.

³⁶ But now, assuredly, thus said the LORD, the God of Israel, concerning this city of which you say, "It is being delivered into the hands of the king of Babylon through the sword, through fam-

---
ᶜ⁻ᶜExact force of Heb uncertain
ᵈ⁻ᵈWith many mss. and ancient versions; other mss. and printed editions read "who wrote"
ᵉ⁻ᵉLit. "to this day"

JEREMIAH 32·37

ine, and through pestilence": ³⁷ See, I will gather them from all the lands to which I have banished them in My anger and wrath, and in great rage; and I will bring them back to this place and let them dwell secure. ³⁸ They shall be My people, and I will be their God. ³⁹ I will give them a single heart and a single nature to revere Me for all time, and it shall be well with them and their children after them. ⁴⁰ And I will make an everlasting covenant with them that I will not turn away from them and that I will treat them kindly; and I will put into their hearts reverence for Me, so that they do not turn away from Me. ⁴¹ I will delight in treating them kindly, and I will plant them in this land faithfully, with all My heart and soul.

⁴² For thus said the LORD: As I have brought this terrible disaster upon this people, so I am going to bring upon them the vast good fortune which I have promised for them. ⁴³ And fields shall again be purchased in this land of which you say, "It is a desolation, without man or beast; it is delivered into the hands of the Chaldeans."
⁴⁴ Fields shall be purchased, and deeds written and sealed, and witnesses called, in the land of Benjamin and in the environs of Jerusalem, and in the towns of Judah; the towns of the hill country, the towns of the Shephelah, and the towns of the Negeb. For I will restore their fortunes—declares the LORD.

33

¹ The word of the LORD came to Jeremiah a second time, while he was still confined in the prison compound, as follows:

² Thus said the LORD who is planning it,
  The LORD who is shaping it to bring it about,
  Whose name is LORD:
³ Call to Me, and I will answer you,
  And I will tell you wondrous things,
  Secrets you have not known.

⁴ For thus said the LORD, the God of Israel, concerning the houses of this city and the palaces of the kings of Judah that were torn down ᵃ⁻for [defense] against the siege-mounds and against the sword, ⁵ and were filled by those who went to fight the Chaldeans,⁻ᵃ with the corpses of the men whom I struck down in My anger and rage, hiding My face from this city because of all their wickedness: ⁶ I am going to bring her relief and healing. I will heal them and reveal to them abundanceᵃ of true peace. ⁷ And I will restore the fortunes of Judah and Israel, and I will rebuild them as of old. ⁸ And I will purge them of all the sins which they committed against Me, and I will pardon all the sins which they committed against Me, by which they rebelled against Me. ⁹ And she shall gain through Me renown, joy, fame, and glory above all the nations on earth, when they hear of all the good fortune I provide for them.ᵇ They will thrill and quiver because of all the good fortune and all the prosperity that I provide for her.

¹⁰ Thus said the LORD: Again there shall be heard in this place, which you say is ruined, without man or beast—in the towns of Judah and the streets of Jerusalem that are desolate, without man, without inhabitants, without beast— ¹¹ the sound of mirth and gladness, the voice of bridegroom and bride, the voice of those who cry, "Give thanks to the LORD of Hosts, for the LORD is good, for His kindness is everlasting!" as they bring thanksgiving offerings to the House of the LORD. For I will restore the fortunes of the land as of old—said the LORD.
¹² Thus said the LORD of Hosts: In this ruined place, without man and beast, and in all its towns, there shall again be a pasture for shepherds, where they can rest their flocks. ¹³ In the towns of the hill country, in the towns of the Shephelah, and in the towns of the Negeb, in the land of Benjamin and in the environs of Jerusalem and in the towns of Judah, sheep shall pass again under the hands of one who counts them—said the LORD. ¹⁴ See, days are coming—declares the LORD—when I will fulfill the promise which I made concerning the House of Israel and the House of Judah. ¹⁵ In

ᵃ⁻ᵃMeaning of Heb uncertain
ᵇI.e. for Israel

those days and at that time, I will raise up for David a righteous descendant,[c] and he shall do what is just and right in the land. 16 In those days Judah shall be delivered and Israel shall dwell securely. And this is what she shall be called: "The LORD is our Vindicator." 17 For thus said the LORD: There shall never be an end to men of David's line who sit upon the throne of the House of Israel. 18 Nor shall there ever be an end to the line of the levitical priests before Me, of those who present burnt offerings and turn the meal offering to smoke and perform sacrifices.

19 The word of the LORD came to Jeremiah: 20 Thus said the LORD: If you could break My covenant with the day and My covenant with the night, so that day and night should not come at their proper time, 21 only then could My covenant with My servant David be broken—so that he would not have a descendant reigning upon his throne—or with My ministrants, the levitical priests. 22 Like the host of heaven which cannot be counted, and the sand of the sea which cannot be measured, so will I multiply the offspring of My servant David, and of the Levites who minister to Me.

23 The word of the LORD came to Jeremiah: 24 You see what this people said: "The two families which the LORD chose have now been rejected by Him." Thus they despise My people, [a-]and regard them as no longer a nation.[-a] 25 Thus said the LORD: As surely as I have established My covenant with day and night—the laws of heaven and earth— 26 so I will never reject the offspring of Jacob and My servant David; I will never fail to take from his offspring rulers for the descendants of Abraham, Isaac, and Jacob. Indeed, I will restore their fortunes and take them back in love.

34

1 The word which came to Jeremiah from the LORD, when King Nebuchadrezzar and all his army, and all the kingdoms of the earth and all the peoples under his sway, were waging war against Jerusalem and all its towns:
2 Thus said the LORD: Go speak to King Zedekiah of Judah, and say to him: Thus said the LORD: I am going to deliver this city into the hands of the king of Babylon, and he will destroy it by fire. 3 And you will not escape from him; you will be captured and handed over to him. [a-]And you will see the king of Babylon face to face and speak to him in person;[-a] and you will be brought to Babylon. 4 But hear the word of the LORD, O King Zedekiah of Judah! Thus said the LORD concerning you: You will not die by the sword. 5 You will die a peaceful death; and as incense[b] was burned for your ancestors, the earlier kings who preceded you, so they will burn incense[b] for you, and they will lament for you "Ah, lord!" For I Myself have made the promise—declares the LORD.
6 The prophet Jeremiah spoke all these words to King Zedekiah of Judah in Jerusalem, 7 when the army of the king of Babylon was waging war against Jerusalem and against the remaining towns of Judah—against Lachish and Azekah, for they were the only fortified towns of Judah that were left.

8 The word which came to Jeremiah from the LORD after King Zedekiah had made a covenant with all the people in Jerusalem to proclaim a release[c] among them— 9 that everyone should set free his Hebrew slaves, both male and female, and that no one should keep his fellow Judean enslaved.
10 Everyone, officers and people, who had entered into the covenant agreed to set their male and female slaves free and not keep them enslaved any longer; they complied and let them go. 11 But afterward they turned about and brought back the men and women they had set free, and forced them into slavery again. 12 Then it was that the word of the LORD came to Jeremiah from the LORD:
13 Thus said the LORD, the God of Israel: I made a covenant with your fathers when I brought them out of the land of Egypt, the house of bondage,

---

[a-a] Meaning of Heb uncertain   [c] Lit. "sprout"
[a-a] For the idiom see note at 32.4
[b] Lit. "burnings"   [c] Others "liberty"

JEREMIAH 34·14

saying: ¹⁴ "In the seventh year[d] each of you must let go any fellow Hebrew [e-who may be sold-e] to you; when he has served you six years, you must set him free." But your fathers would not obey Me or give ear. ¹⁵ Lately you turned about and did what is proper in My sight, and each of you proclaimed a release to his countrymen; and you made a covenant accordingly before Me in the House which bears My name. ¹⁶ But now you have turned back and have profaned My name; each of you has brought back the men and women whom you had given their freedom, and forced them to be your slaves again.

¹⁷ Assuredly, thus said the LORD: You would not obey Me and proclaim a release, each to his kinsman and countryman. Lo! I proclaim your release —declares the LORD—to the sword, to pestilence, and to famine; and I will make you a horror to all the kingdoms of the earth. ¹⁸ I will make the men who violated My covenant, who did not fulfill the terms of the covenant which they made before Me, [like] the calf which they cut in two so as to pass between the halves[f]— ¹⁹ the officers of Judah and Jerusalem, the officials, the priests, and all the people of the land who passed between the halves of the calf, ²⁰ shall be handed over to their enemies, to those who seek to kill them. Their carcasses shall become food for the birds of the sky and the beasts of the earth. ²¹ I will hand over King Zedekiah of Judah and his officers to their enemies, who seek to kill them—to the army of the king of Babylon which has withdrawn from you. ²² I hereby give the command—declares the LORD— by which I will bring them back against this city. They shall attack it and capture it, and burn it down. I will make the towns of Judah a desolation, without inhabitant.

35

¹ The word which came to Jeremiah from the LORD in the days of King Jehoiakim son of Josiah of Judah:

² Go to the house of the Rechabites and speak to them, and bring them to the House of the LORD, to one of the chambers, and give them wine to drink.

³ So I took Jaazaniah son of Jeremiah son of Habazziniah, and his brothers, all his sons, and the whole household of the Rechabites; ⁴ and I brought them to the House of the LORD, to the chamber of the sons of Hanan son of Igdaliah, the man of God, which is next to the chamber of the officials and above the chamber of Maaseiah son of Shallum, the guardian of the threshold. ⁵ I set goblets and cups of wine before the men of the house of the Rechabites, and said to them, "Have some wine."

⁶ They replied. "We will not drink wine, for our ancestor, Jonadab son of Rechab, commanded us: 'You shall never drink wine, either you or your children. ⁷ Nor shall you build houses or sow fields[a] or plant vineyards, nor shall you own such things; but you shall live in tents all your days, so that you may live long upon the land where you sojourn.' ⁸ And we have obeyed our ancestor Jonadab son of Rechab in all that he commanded us: we never drink wine, neither we nor our wives nor our sons and daughters. ⁹ Nor do we build houses to live in, and we do not own vineyards or fields for sowing; ¹⁰ but we live in tents. We have obeyed and done all that our ancestor Jonadab commanded us. ¹¹ But when King Nebuchadrezzar of Babylon invaded the country, we said, 'Come, let us go into Jerusalem because of the army of the Chaldeans and the army of Aram.' And so we are living in Jerusalem."

¹² Then the word of the Lord came to Jeremiah: ¹³ Thus said the LORD of Hosts, the God of Israel: Go say to the men of Judah and the inhabitants of Jerusalem: You can learn a lesson [here] about obeying My commands—declares the LORD. ¹⁴ The commands of Jonadab son of Rechab have been fulfilled: he charged his children not to drink wine,

---

[d] I.e. of servitude. Lit. "After a period of seven years"; cf. Deut. 14.28 and 15.1
[e-e] Or "who sells himself"
[f] Cf. Gen. 15.9–10, 17–21

[a] Lit. "seed"

JEREMIAH 35·15

and to this day they have not drunk, in obedience to the charge of their ancestor. But I spoke to you persistently, and you did not listen to Me. ¹⁵ I persistently sent you all My servants, the prophets, to say: "Turn back, every one of you, from your wicked ways and mend your deeds; do not follow other gods or serve them. Then you may remain on the land which I gave to you and your fathers." But you did not give ear or listen to Me. ¹⁶ The family of Jonadab son of Rechab have indeed fulfilled the charge which their ancestor gave them; but this people has not listened to Me. ¹⁷ Assuredly, thus said the LORD, the God of Hosts, the God of Israel: I am going to bring upon Judah and upon all the inhabitants of Jerusalem all the disaster with which I have threatened them; for I spoke to them, but they would not listen; I called to them, but they would not respond.

¹⁸ And to the family of the Rechabites Jeremiah said: Thus said the LORD of Hosts, the God of Israel: Because you obeyed the charge of your ancestor Jonadab, and all his commandments and did all that he enjoined upon you, ¹⁹ assuredly, thus said the LORD of Hosts, the God of Israel: There shall never cease to be a man of the line of Jonadab son of Rechab standing before Me.

36

¹ In the fourth year of King Jehoiakim son of Josiah of Judah, this word came to Jeremiah from the LORD:

² "Get a scroll and write upon it all the words that I have spoken to you—concerning Israel and Judah and all the nations—from the time I first spoke to you in the days of Josiah to this day. ³ Perhaps when the House of Judah hear of all the disasters I intend to bring upon them, they will turn back from their wicked ways, and I will pardon their iniquity and their sin." ⁴ So Jeremiah called Baruch son of Neriah; and Baruch wrote down in the scroll, at Jeremiah's dictation, all the words which the LORD had spoken to him.

⁵ Jeremiah instructed Baruch, "I am in hiding; I cannot go to the House of the LORD. ⁶ But you go and read aloud the words of the LORD from the scroll which you wrote at my dictation, to all the people in the House of the LORD on a fast day; thus you will also be reading them to all the Judeans who come in from the towns. ⁷ Perhaps their entreaty will be accepted by the LORD, if they turn back from their wicked ways. For great is the anger and wrath with which the LORD has threatened this people."

⁸ Baruch son of Neriah did just as the prophet Jeremiah had instructed him, about reading the words of the LORD from the scroll in the House of the LORD. ⁹ In the ninth month of the fifth year of King Jehoiakim son of Josiah of Judah, all the people in Jerusalem and all the people coming from Judah proclaimed a fast before the LORD in Jerusalem. ¹⁰ It was then that Baruch—in the chamber of Gemariah son of Shaphan the scribe, in the upper court, near the new gateway of the House of the LORD—read the words of Jeremiah from the scroll to all the people in the House of the LORD.

¹¹ Micaiah son of Gemariah son of Shaphan heard all the words of the LORD [read] from the scroll, ¹² and he went down to the king's palace, to the chamber of the scribe. There he found all the officials in session: Elishama the scribe, Delaiah son of Shemaiah, Elnathan son of Achbor, Gemariah son of Shaphan, Zedekiah son of Hananiah, and all the other officials. ¹³ And Micaiah told them all that he had heard as Baruch read from the scroll in the hearing of the people.

¹⁴ Then all the officials sent Jehudi son of Nethaniah son of Shelemiah son of Cushi to say to Baruch, "Take that scroll from which you read to the people, and come along!" And Baruch took the scroll and came to them.

¹⁵ They said, ᵃ⁻"Sit down and read it⁻ᵃ to us." And Baruch read it to them. ¹⁶ When they heard all these words, they turned to each other in fear; and they said to Baruch, "We must report all this to the king."

ᵃ⁻ᵃ Change of vocalization yields "Read it again"; cf. Targum and Septuagint

JEREMIAH 36·17

¹⁷ And they questioned Baruch further, "Tell us how you wrote down all these words ᵇ-that he spoke."-ᵇ ¹⁸ He answered them, "He himself recited all those words to me, and I wrote them down in the scroll in ink."

¹⁹ The officials said to Baruch, "Go into hiding, you and Jeremiah. Let no man know where you are!" ²⁰ And they went to the king in the court, after leaving the scroll in the chamber of the scribe Elishama. And they reported all these matters to the king.

²¹ The king sent Jehudi to get the scroll and Jehudi fetched the scroll from the chamber of the scribe Elishama. Jehudi read it to the king and to all the officials who were in attendance on the king. ²² Since it was the ninth month, the king was sitting in the winter house, with a fire burning in the brazier before him. ²³ And every time Jehudi read three or four columns, he would cut it up with a scribe's knife and throw it into the fire in the brazier, until the entire scroll was consumed by the fire in the brazier. ²⁴ Yet the king and all his courtiers who heard all these words showed no fear and did not tear their garments; ²⁵ moreover, Elnathan, Delaiah, and Gemariah begged the king not to burn the scroll, but he would not listen to them.

²⁶ The king ordered Jerahmeel, the king's son, and Seraiah son of Azriel, and Shelemiah son of Abdeel to arrest the scribe Baruch and the prophet Jeremiah. But the LORD hid them.

²⁷ The word of the LORD came to Jeremiah after the king had burned the scroll containing the words that Baruch had written at Jeremiah's dictation: ²⁸ Get yourself another scroll, and write upon it the same words that were in the first scroll which was burned by King Jehoiakim of Judah. ²⁹ And concerning King Jehoiakim of Judah you shall say: Thus said the LORD: You burned that scroll, saying, "How dare you write in it that the king of Babylon will come and destroy this land and cause man and beast to cease from it?" ³⁰ Assuredly, thus said the LORD concerning King Jehoiakim of Judah: He shall not have any of his line sitting on the throne of David; and his own corpse shall be left exposed to the heat by day and the cold by night. ³¹ And I will punish him and his offspring and his courtiers for their iniquity; I will bring on them and on the inhabitants of Jerusalem and on all the men of Judah all the disasters of which I have warned them—but they would not listen.

³² So Jeremiah got another scroll and gave it to the scribe Baruch son of Neriah. And at Jeremiah's dictation, he wrote in it the whole text of the scroll which King Jehoiakim of Judah had burned, and much more of the like.

37

¹ Zedekiah son of Josiah became king instead of Coniah son of Jehoiakim, for King Nebuchadrezzar of Babylon set him up as king over the land of Judah. ² Neither he nor his courtiers nor the people of the land gave heed to the words which the LORD spoke through the prophet Jeremiah.

³ Yet King Zedekiah sent Jehucal son of Shelemiah and Zephaniah son of Maaseiah the priest to the prophet Jeremiah, to say, "Please pray on our behalf to the LORD our God." ⁴ (Jeremiah could still go in and out among the people, for they had not yet put him in prison. ⁵ The army of Pharaoh had set out from Egypt; and when the Chaldeans who were besieging Jerusalem heard the report, they raised the siege of Jerusalem.)

⁶ Then the word of the LORD came to the prophet Jeremiah: ⁷ Thus said the LORD, the God of Israel: Thus shall you say to the king of Judah who sent you to Me to inquire of Me: The army of Pharaoh, which set out to help you, will return to its own land, to Egypt. ⁸ And the Chaldeans will come back and attack this city and they will capture it and destroy it by fire.

⁹ Thus said the LORD: Do not delude yourselves into thinking, "The Chaldeans will go away from

ᵇ⁻ᵇ Force of Heb uncertain

JEREMIAH 37.10

us." They will not go away. ¹⁰ Even if you defeated the whole army of the Chaldeans that are fighting against you, and only wounded men were left lying in their tents, they would get up and burn this city down!

¹¹ When the army of the Chaldeans raised the siege of Jerusalem on account of the army of Pharaoh, ¹² Jeremiah was going to leave Jerusalem and go to the territory of Benjamin ᵃ⁻to share in some property thereᵃ among the people. ¹³ When he got to the Benjamin Gate, there was a guard officer there named Irijah son of Shelemiah son of Hananiah; and he arrested Jeremiah, saying, "You are defecting to the Chaldeans!" ¹⁴ Jeremiah answered, "That's a lie! I'm not defecting to the Chaldeans!" But Irijah would not listen to him; he arrested Jeremiah and brought him to the officials. ¹⁵ The officials were furious with Jeremiah; they beat him and put him into prison, in the house of the scribe Jonathan—for it had been made into a jail. ¹⁶ Thus Jeremiah came to the ᵃ⁻pit and the cells,⁻ᵃ and Jeremiah remained there a long time.

¹⁷ Then King Zedekiah sent for him, and the king questioned him secretly in his palace. He asked, "Is there any word from the LORD?" "There is!" Jeremiah answered, and he continued, "You will be delivered into the hands of the king of Babylon."

¹⁸ And Jeremiah said to King Zedekiah, "What wrong have I done to you, to your courtiers, and to this people, that you have put me in jail? ¹⁹ And where are those prophets of yours who prophesied to you that the king of Babylon would never move against you and against this land? ²⁰ Now, please hear me, my lord king, and grant my plea: Don't send me back to the house of the scribe Jonathan ᵇ⁻to die there."⁻ᵇ

²¹ So King Zedekiah gave instructions to lodge Jeremiah in the prison compound and to supply him daily with a loaf of bread from the Bakers' Street—until all the bread in the city was gone. Jeremiah remained in the prison compound.

38

¹ Shephatiah son of Mattan, Gedaliah son of Pashhur, Jucal son of Shelemiah, and Pashhur son of Malchiah heard what Jeremiah was saying to all the people: ² "Thus said the LORD: Whoever remains in this city shall die by the sword, by famine, and by pestilence; but whoever surrenders to the Chaldeans shall live; ᵃ⁻he shall at least gain his life⁻ᵃ and shall live. ³ Thus said the LORD: This city shall be delivered into the hands of the king of Babylon's army, and he shall capture it."

⁴ Then the officials said to the king, "Let that man be put to death, for he disheartensᵇ the soldiers, and all the people who are left in this city, by speaking such things to them. That man is not seeking the welfare of this people, but their harm!" ⁵ King Zedekiah replied, "He is in your hands; the king cannot oppose you in anything!"

⁶ So they took Jeremiah and put him down in the pit of Malchiah, the king's son, which was in the prison compound; they let Jeremiah down by ropes. There was no water in the pit, only mud, and Jeremiah sank into the mud.

⁷ Ebed-melech the Ethiopian, a eunuch who was in the king's palace, heard that they had put Jeremiah in the pit. The king was then sitting at the Benjamin Gate; ⁸ so Ebed-melech left the king's palace, and spoke to the king: ⁹ "My lord king, those men have acted wickedly in all they did to the prophet Jeremiah; they have put him down in the pit, to die there of hunger." For there was no more bread in the city.

¹⁰ Then the king instructed Ebed-melech the Ethiopian, "Take with you thirtyᶜ men from here, and pull the prophet Jeremiah up from the pit before he dies." ¹¹ So Ebed-melech took the men with him, and went to the king's palace, to ᵈ⁻a place below⁻ᵈ the treasury. There they got worn cloths and rags, which they let down to Jeremiah in the

---

ᵃ⁻ᵃ Meaning of Heb uncertain
ᵇ⁻ᵇ Lit. "and let me not die there"

ᵃ⁻ᵃ Lit. "he shall have his life as booty"; cf. 21.9
ᵇ Lit. "weakens the hands of"
ᶜ One ms. reads "three"
ᵈ⁻ᵈ Emendation yields "the wardrobe of"

JEREMIAH 38.12

pit by ropes. ¹² And Ebed-melech the Ethiopian called to Jeremiah, "Put the worn cloths and rags under your armpits, inside the ropes." Jeremiah did so, ¹³ and they pulled Jeremiah up by the ropes and got him out of the pit. And Jeremiah remained in the prison compound.

¹⁴ King Zedekiah sent for the prophet Jeremiah, and had him brought to him at the third entrance of the House of the LORD. And the king said to Jeremiah, "I want to ask you something; don't conceal anything from me."
¹⁵ Jeremiah answered the king, "If I tell you, you'll surely kill me; and if I give you advice, you won't listen to me."
¹⁶ Thereupon King Zedekiah secretly promised Jeremiah on oath: "As the LORD lives who has ᵉ⁻given us this life,⁻ᵉ I will not put you to death or leave you in the hands of those men who seek your life."
¹⁷ Then Jeremiah said to Zedekiah, "Thus said the LORD of Hosts, the God of Israel: If you surrender to the officers of the king of Babylon, your life will be spared and this city will not be burned down. You and your household will live. ¹⁸ But if you do not surrender to the officers of the king of Babylon, this city will be delivered into the hands of the Chaldeans, who will burn it down; and you will not escape from them."
¹⁹ King Zedekiah said to Jeremiah, "I am worried about the Judeans who have defected to the Chaldeans; that they [the Chaldeans] might hand me over to them to abuse me."
²⁰ "They will not hand you over," Jeremiah replied. "Listen to the voice of the LORD, to what I tell you, that it may go well with you and your life be spared. ²¹ For this is what the LORD has shown me if you refuse to surrender: ²² All the women who are left in the palace of the king of Judah shall be brought out to the officers of the king of Babylon; and they shall say:

The men who were your friends
Have seduced you and vanquished you.
Now that your feet are sunk in the mire,
They have turned their backs [on you].

²³ They will bring out all your wives and children to the Chaldeans, and you yourself will not escape from them. You will be captured by the king of Babylon, and ᶠ⁻this city shall be burned down."⁻ᶠ

²⁴ Zedekiah said to Jeremiah, "Don't let anyone know about this conversation, ᵍ⁻or you will die.⁻ᵍ ²⁵ If the officials should hear that I have spoken with you, and they should come and say to you, 'Tell us what you said to the king; hide nothing from us, ʰ⁻or we'll kill you.⁻ʰ And what did the king say to you?' ²⁶ say to them, 'I was presenting my petition to the king not to send me back to the house of Jonathan to die there.'"
²⁷ All the officials did come to Jeremiah to question him; and he replied to them just as the king had instructed him. So they stopped questioning him, for the conversation had not been overheard.
²⁸ Jeremiah remained in the prison compound until the day Jerusalem was captured.
When Jerusalem was captured . . .ⁱ

39

¹ In the ninth year of King Zedekiah of Judah, in the tenth month, King Nebuchadrezzar of Babylon moved against Jerusalem with his whole army, and they laid siege to it. ² And in the eleventh year of Zedekiah, on the ninth day of the fourth month, the [walls of] the city were breached. ³ All the officers of the king of Babylon entered, and took up quarters at the middle gate—Nergal-sarezer, Samgar-nebo, Sarsechim the Rab-saris,ᵃ Nergal-sarezer the Rab-mag,ᵃ and all the rest of the officers of the king of Babylon.
⁴ When King Zedekiah of Judah saw them, he and all the soldiers fled. They left the city at night, by way of the king's garden, through the gate between the double walls; and he set out toward the

---

ᵉ⁻ᵉ Meaning of Heb uncertain
ᶠ⁻ᶠ So Targum and Septuagint and some mss. Most mss. and editions read "you will burn down this city by fire"
ᵍ⁻ᵍ Lit. "that you may not die"
ʰ⁻ʰ Lit. "that we may not kill you"
ⁱ This clause would read well before 39.3

ᵃ Titles of officers

JEREMIAH 39.5

Arabah.[b] ⁵ But the Chaldean troops pursued them, and they overtook Zedekiah in the steppes of Jericho. They captured him and brought him before King Nebuchadrezzar of Babylon at Riblah in the region of Hamath; and he put him on trial. ⁶ The king of Babylon had Zedekiah's children slaughtered at Riblah before his eyes; the king of Babylon also had all the nobles of Judah slaughtered. ⁷ Then the eyes of Zedekiah were put out and he was chained in bronze fetters, that he might be brought to Babylon.

⁸ The Chaldeans burned down the king's palace and the houses[c] of the people by fire, and they tore down the walls of Jerusalem. ⁹ The rest of the people who remained in the city, and the defectors who had gone over to him—the rest of the people who remained—were exiled by Nebuzaradan, the chief of the guards, to Babylon. ¹⁰ But some of the poorest people who owned nothing were left in the land of Judah by Nebuzaradan, the chief of the guards, and he gave them vineyards and fields at that time.

¹¹ King Nebuchadrezzar of Babylon had given orders to Nebuzaradan, the chief of the guards, concerning Jeremiah: ¹² "Take him and look after him; do him no harm, but grant whatever he asks of you." ¹³ So Nebuzaradan, the chief of the guards, and Nebushazban the Rab-saris, and Nergal-sarezer the Rab-mag, and all the commanders of the king of Babylon sent ¹⁴ and had Jeremiah brought from the prison compound. They committed him to the care of Gedaliah son of Ahikam son of Shaphan, [d-]that he might be left at liberty in a house.[-d] So he dwelt among the people.

¹⁵ The word of the LORD had come to Jeremiah while he was still confined in the prison compound: ¹⁶ Go and say to Ebed-melech the Ethiopian: Thus said the LORD of Hosts, the God of Israel: I am going to fulfill My words concerning this city—for disaster, not for good—and they shall come true on that day in your presence. ¹⁷ But I will save you on that day—declares the LORD; you shall not be delivered into the hands of the men you dread. ¹⁸ I will rescue you, and you shall not fall by the sword. [e-]You shall escape with your life,[-e] because you trusted Me—declares the LORD.

40

¹ The word that came to Jeremiah from the LORD, after Nebuzaradan, the chief of the guards, set him free at Ramah, to which he had taken him, chained in fetters, among those from Jerusalem and Judah who were being exiled to Babylon.

² The chief of the guards took charge of Jeremiah, and he said to him, "The LORD your God threatened this place with this disaster; ³ and now the LORD has brought it about. He has acted as He threatened, because you sinned against the LORD and did not obey Him. That is why this has happened to you. ⁴ Now, I release you this day from the fetters which were on your hands. If you would like to go with me to Babylon, come, and I will look after you. And if you don't want to come with me to Babylon, you need not. See, the whole land is before you: go wherever seems good and right to you." ⁵ —[a-]But [Jeremiah] still did not turn back.[-a]—"Or go to Gedaliah son of Ahikam son of Shaphan, whom the king of Babylon has put in charge of the towns of Judah, and stay with him among the people, or go wherever you want to go."

The chief of the guards gave him an allowance of food, and dismissed him. ⁶ So Jeremiah came to Gedaliah son of Ahikam at Mizpah, and stayed with him among the people who were left in the land.

⁷ The officers of the troops in the open country, and their men with them, heard that the king of Babylon had put Gedaliah son of Ahikam in charge of the region, and that he had put in his charge the men, women, and children of the poor folk, those who had not been exiled to Babylon.

[b]Hoping to escape across the Jordan
[c]Taking Heb singular as collective, with Kimhi
[d-d]Meaning of Heb uncertain
[e-e]See note at 21.9; 38.2

[a-a]Meaning of Heb uncertain

JEREMIAH 40·8

⁸ So they with their men came to Gedaliah at Mizpah—Ishmael son of Nethaniah; Johanan and Jonathan the sons of Kareah; Seraiah son of Tanhumeth; the sons of Ephai the Netophathite; and Jezaniah son of the Maacathite. ⁹ Gedaliah son of Ahikam son of Shaphan reassured[b] them and their men, saying, "Do not be afraid to serve the Chaldeans. Stay in the land and serve the king of Babylon, and it will go well with you. ¹⁰ I am going to stay in Mizpah to attend upon the Chaldeans who will come to us. But you may gather wine and fruit and oil and put them in your own vessels, and settle in the towns you have occupied."

¹¹ Likewise, all the Judeans who were in Moab, Ammon, and Edom, or who were in other lands, heard that the king of Babylon had let a remnant stay in Judah, and that he had put Gedaliah son of Ahikam son of Shaphan in charge of them. ¹² All these Judeans returned from all the places to which they had scattered. They came to the land of Judah, to Gedaliah at Mizpah, and they gathered large quantities of wine and summer fruit.

¹³ Johanan son of Kareah, and all the officers of the troops in the open country, came to Gedaliah at Mizpah ¹⁴ and said to him, "Do you know that King Baalis of Ammon has sent Ishmael son of Nethaniah to kill you?" But Gedaliah son of Ahikam would not believe them. ¹⁵ Johanan son of Kareah also said secretly to Gedaliah at Mizpah, "Let me go and strike down Ishmael son of Nethaniah before anyone knows about it; otherwise he will kill you, and all the Judeans who have gathered about you will be dispersed, and the remnant of Judah will perish!"

¹⁶ But Gedaliah son of Ahikam answered Johanan son of Kareah, "Do not do such a thing: what you are saying about Ishmael is not true!"

41

¹ In the seventh month, Ishmael son of Nethaniah son of Elishama, who was of royal descent and one of the king's commanders, came with ten men to Gedaliah son of Ahikam at Mizpah; and they ate together there at Mizpah. ² Then Ishmael son of Nethaniah and the ten men who were with him arose and struck down Gedaliah son of Ahikam son of Shaphan with the sword and killed him, because the king of Babylon had put him in charge of the land. ³ Ishmael also killed all the Judeans who were with him—with Gedaliah in Mizpah—and the Chaldean soldiers who were stationed there.

⁴ The second day after Gedaliah was killed, when no one yet knew about it, ⁵ eighty men came from Shechem, Shiloh, and Samaria, their beards shaved, their garments torn, and their bodies gashed, carrying meal offerings and frankincense to present at the House of the LORD. ⁶ Ishmael son of Nethaniah went out from Mizpah to meet them, weeping as he walked. As he met them, he said to them, "Come to Gedaliah son of Ahikam." ⁷ When they came inside the town, Ishmael son of Nethaniah and the men who were with him slaughtered them [and threw their bodies] into a cistern.

⁸ But there were ten men among them who said to Ishmael, "Don't kill us! We have stores hidden in a field—wheat, barley, oil, and honey." So he stopped, and did not kill them along with their fellows.— ⁹ The cistern into which Ishmael threw all the corpses of the men he had killed in the affair of Gedaliah was the one that King Asa had constructed on account of King Baasha of Israel. That was the one which Ishmael son of Nethaniah filled with corpses.— ¹⁰ Ishmael carried off all the rest of the people who were in Mizpah, including the daughters of the king—all the people left in Mizpah, over whom Nebuzaradan, the chief of the guards, had appointed Gedaliah son of Ahikam. Ishmael son of Nethaniah carried them off, and set out to cross over to the Ammonites.

¹¹ Johanan son of Kareah, and all the army officers with him, heard of all the crimes committed by Ishmael son of Nethaniah. ¹² They took all their men and went to fight against Ishmael son of Nethaniah; and they encountered him by the great pool in Gibeon. ¹³ When all the people held by Ishmael saw Johanan son of Kareah and all the

---

[b] Lit. "swore to"

JEREMIAH 41.14

army officers with him, they were glad; ¹⁴ all the people whom Ishmael had carried off from Mizpah turned back and went over to Johanan son of Kareah. ¹⁵ But Ishmael son of Nethaniah escaped from Johanan with eight men, and went to the Ammonites.

¹⁶ Johanan son of Kareah and all the army officers with him took all the rest of the people whom *ᵃ-*he had rescued from Ishmael son of Nethaniah*-ᵃ* from Mizpah after he had murdered Gedaliah son of Ahikam—the men, soldiers, women, children, and eunuchs whom [Johanan] had brought back from Gibeon. ¹⁷ They set out, and they stopped at Geruth*ᵇ* Chimham, near Bethlehem, on their way to go to Egypt ¹⁸ because of the Chaldeans. For they were afraid of them, because Ishmael son of Nethaniah had killed Gedaliah son of Ahikam, whom the king of Babylon had put in charge of the land.

42

¹ Then all the army officers, with Johanan son of Kareah, Jezaniah son of Hoshaiah, and all the rest of the people, great and small, approached ² the prophet Jeremiah and said, "Grant our plea, and pray for us to the LORD your God, for all this remnant! For we remain but a few out of many, as you can see. ³ Let the LORD your God tell us where we should go and what we should do."

⁴ The prophet Jeremiah answered them, "Agreed: I will pray to the LORD your God as you request, and I will tell you whatever response the LORD gives for you. I will withhold nothing from you."

⁵ Thereupon they said to Jeremiah, "Let the LORD be a true and faithful witness against us! We swear that we will do exactly as the LORD your God instructs us through you! ⁶ Whether it is pleasant or unpleasant, we will obey the LORD our God to whom we send you, in order that it may go well with us when we obey the LORD our God."

⁷ After ten days, the word of the LORD came to Jeremiah. ⁸ He called Johanan son of Kareah and all the army officers, and the rest of the people, great and small, ⁹ and said to them, "Thus said the LORD, the God of Israel, to whom you sent me to present your supplication before Him: ¹⁰ If you remain in this land, I will build you and not overthrow, I will plant you and not uproot; for I regret the punishment I have brought upon you. ¹¹ Do not be afraid of the king of Babylon, whom you fear; do not be afraid of him—declares the LORD—for I am with you to save you and to rescue you from his hands. ¹² I will dispose him to be merciful to you: he shall show you mercy and *ᵃ-*bring you back to*-ᵃ* your own land.

¹³ "But if you say, We will not stay in this land—thus disobeying the LORD your God— ¹⁴ if you say, No! We will go to the land of Egypt, so that we may not see war nor hear the sound of the horn, and so that we may not hunger for bread; there we will stay, ¹⁵ then hear the word of the LORD, O remnant of Judah! Thus said the LORD of Hosts, the God of Israel: If you turn your faces toward Egypt, and you go and sojourn there, ¹⁶ the sword that you fear shall overtake you in the land of Egypt, and the famine you worry over shall follow at your heels in Egypt too; and there you shall die. ¹⁷ All the men who turn their faces toward Egypt, in order to sojourn there, shall die by the sword, by famine, and by pestilence. They shall have no surviving remnant of the disaster which I will bring upon them. ¹⁸ For thus said the LORD of Hosts, the God of Israel: As My anger and wrath were poured out upon the inhabitants of Jerusalem, so will My wrath be poured out on you if you go to Egypt. You shall become *ᵇ-*an execration of woe, a curse*-ᵇ* and a mockery; and you shall never again see this place. ¹⁹ The LORD has spoken against you, O remnant of Judah! Do not go to Egypt! Know well, then—for I warn you this day ²⁰ that you were deceitful at heart when you sent me to the LORD your God, saying, 'Pray for us to the LORD our God; and whatever the LORD our God may say, just tell us and we will do

---

*ᵃ⁻ᵃ*Emendation yields "Ishmael son of Nethaniah had carried off"
*ᵇ*Aquila reads "the sheepfolds of"

*ᵃ⁻ᵃ*Change of vocalization yields "let you dwell in"
*ᵇ⁻ᵇ*I.e. a standard by which men execrate and curse; cf. note at 24.9

JEREMIAH 42·21

it.' ²¹ I told you today, and you have not obeyed the Lord your God in respect to all that He sent me to tell you— ²² know well, then, that you shall die by the sword, by famine, and by pestilence in the place where you want to go and sojourn."

43

¹ When Jeremiah had finished speaking all these words to all the people—all the words of the Lord their God, with which the Lord their God had sent him to them— ² Azariah son of Hoshaiah and Johanan son of Kareah and all the arrogant men said to Jeremiah, "You are lying! The Lord our God did not send you to say, 'Don't go to Egypt and sojourn there'! ³ It is Baruch son of Neriah who is inciting you against us, so that we will be delivered into the hands of the Chaldeans to be killed or to be exiled to Babylon!"

⁴ So Johanan son of Kareah and all the army officers and the rest of the people did not obey the Lord's command to remain in the land of Judah. ⁵ Instead, Johanan son of Kareah and all the army officers took the entire remnant of Judah—those who had returned from all the countries to which they had been scattered and had sojourned in the land of Judah, ⁶ men, women, and children; and the daughters of the king and all the people whom Nebuzaradan the chief of the guards had left with Gedaliah son of Ahikam son of Shaphan, as well as the prophet Jeremiah and Baruch son of Neriah — ⁷ and they went to Egypt. They did not obey the Lord.

They arrived at Tahpanhes, ⁸ and the word of the Lord came to Jeremiah in Tahpanhes:

⁹ Get yourself large stones, and embed them in mortar in the brick structure at the entrance to Pharaoh's palace in Tahpanhes, with some Judeans looking on. ¹⁰ And say to them: Thus said the Lord of Hosts, the God of Israel: I am sending for My servant King Nebuchadrezzar of Babylon, and I^a will set his throne over these stones which I have

embedded. He will spread out his pavilion^b over them. ¹¹ He will come and attack the land of Egypt, delivering

Those destined for the plague, to the plague,
Those destined for captivity, to captivity,
And those destined for the sword, to the sword.

¹² And I^a will set fire to the temples of the gods of Egypt; he will burn them down and carry them^c off. He shall wrap himself up in the land of Egypt, as a shepherd wraps himself up in his garment. And he shall depart from there in safety. ¹³ He shall smash the obelisks of the Temple of the Sun which is in the land of Egypt, and he shall burn down the temples of the gods of Egypt.

^aSeptuagint reads "he"
^bMeaning of Heb uncertain
^cI.e. the gods

44

¹ The word which came to Jeremiah for all the Judeans living in the land of Egypt, living in Migdol, Tahpanhes, and Noph, and in the land of Pathros:

² Thus said the LORD of Hosts, the God of Israel: You have seen all the disaster that I brought on Jerusalem and on all the towns of Judah. They are a ruin today, and no one inhabits them, ³ on account of the wicked things they did to vex Me, going to make offerings in worship of other gods which they had not known—neither they nor you nor your fathers. ⁴ Yet I persistently sent to you all My servants the prophets, to say to you, "I beg you not to do this abominable thing which I hate." ⁵ But they would not listen or give ear, to turn back from their wickedness and not make offerings to other gods; ⁶ so My fierce anger was poured out, and it blazed against the towns of Judah and the streets of Jerusalem. And they became a desolate ruin, as they still are today

⁷ And now, thus said the LORD, the God of Hosts, the God of Israel: Why are you doing such great harm to yourselves, so that every man and woman, child and infant of yours shall be cut off from the midst of Judah, and no remnant shall be left of you? ⁸ For you vex me by your deeds, making offering to other gods in the land of Egypt where you have come to sojourn, so that you shall be cut off and become a curse*ᵃ* and a mockery among all the nations of earth. ⁹ Have you forgotten the wicked acts of your forefathers, of the kings of Judah and their*ᵇ* wives, and your own wicked acts and those of your wives, which were committed in the land of Judah and in the streets of Jerusalem? ¹⁰ No one has shown contrition to this day, and no one has shown reverence. You*ᶜ* have not followed the Teaching and the laws which I set before you and before your fathers.

¹¹ Assuredly, thus said the LORD of Hosts, the God of Israel: I am going to set My face against you for punishment, to cut off all of Judah. ¹² I will take the remnant of Judah who turned their faces toward the land of Egypt, to go and sojourn there, and they shall be utterly consumed in the land of Egypt. They shall fall by the sword, they shall be consumed by famine; great and small alike shall die by the sword and by famine, and they shall become an execration*ᵃ* and a desolation, a curse*ᵃ* and a mockery.*ᵃ* ¹³ I will punish those who live in the land of Egypt as I punished Jerusalem, with the sword, with famine, and with pestilence. ¹⁴ Of the remnant of Judah who came to sojourn here in the land of Egypt, no survivor or fugitive shall be left to return to the land of Judah. Though they all long to return and dwell there, none shall return except [a few] survivors.

¹⁵ Thereupon they answered Jeremiah—all the men who knew that their wives made offerings to other gods; all the women present, a large gathering; and all the people who lived in Pathros in the land of Egypt: ¹⁶ "We will not listen to you in the matter about which you spoke to us in the name of the LORD. ¹⁷ On the contrary, we will do *ᵈ*-everything which we have vowed-*ᵈ*—to burn incense to the Queen of Heaven and to pour libations to her, as we used to do,*ᵉ* we and our fathers, our kings and our officials, in the towns of Judah and the streets of Jerusalem. For then we had plenty to eat, we were well-off, and suffered no misfortune. ¹⁸ But ever since we stopped burning incense to the Queen of Heaven and pouring libations to her, we have lacked everything, and we have been consumed by the sword and by famine. ¹⁹ And when we burn incense to the Queen of Heaven and pour libations to her, is it without our husbands' approval that we have made cakes *ᶠ*-in her likeness-*ᶠ* and poured libations to her?"

²⁰ Jeremiah replied to all the people, men and women—all the people who argued with him. He said, ²¹ "Indeed, the incense you burned in the towns of Judah and the streets of Jerusalem—you, your fathers, your kings, your officials, and the people of the land—was remembered by the LORD and brought to mind! ²² When the LORD could no longer bear your evil practices and the abominations you committed, your land became a desolate

---

*ᵃ*See note at 24.9; 42.18
*ᵇ*Heb "his"
*ᶜ*Heb "They"
*ᵈ⁻ᵈ*Lit. "everything that has gone forth from our mouth"
*ᵉ*Cf. 7.18
*ᶠ⁻ᶠ*Meaning of Heb uncertain

JEREMIAH 44·23

ruin and a curse,[a] without inhabitant, as is still the case. 23 Because you burned incense and sinned against the LORD and did not obey the LORD, and because you did not follow His Teaching, His laws, and His exhortations, therefore this disaster has befallen you, as is still the case."

24 Jeremiah further said to the people and to all the women: "Hear the word of the LORD, all Judeans in the land of Egypt! 25 Thus said the LORD of Hosts, the God of Israel: You and your wives have [g-]confirmed by deed what you spoke in words:[-g] 'We will fulfill the vows which we made, to burn incense to the Queen of Heaven and to pour libations to her.' So fulfill your vows; perform your vows!

26 "Yet hear the word of the LORD, all Judeans who dwell in the land of Egypt! Lo, I swear by My great name—said the LORD—that none of the men of Judah in all the land of Egypt shall ever again invoke My name, saying, 'As the Lord GOD lives!' 27 I will be watchful over them to their hurt, not to their benefit; all the men of Judah in the land of Egypt shall be consumed by sword and by famine, until they cease to be. 28 Only the few who survive the sword shall return from the land of Egypt to the land of Judah. All the remnant of Judah who came to the land of Egypt to sojourn there shall learn whose word will be fulfilled—Mine or theirs!

29 "And this shall be the sign to you—declares the LORD—that I am going to deal with you in this place, so that you may know that My threats of punishment against you will be fulfilled: 30 Thus said the LORD: I will deliver Pharaoh Hophra, king of Egypt, into the hands of his enemies, those who seek his life, just as I delivered King Zedekiah of Judah into the hands of King Nebuchadrezzar of Babylon, his enemy who sought his life."

45

1 The word which the prophet Jeremiah spoke to Baruch son of Neriah, when he was writing these words in a scroll at Jeremiah's dictation, in the fourth year of King Jehoiakim son of Josiah of Judah:

2 Thus said the LORD, the God of Israel, concerning you, Baruch: 3 You say, "Woe is me! The LORD has added grief to my pain. I am worn out with groaning, and I have found no rest." 4 Thus shall you speak to him: Thus said the LORD: I am going to overthrow what I have built, and uproot what I have planted—[a-]this applies to the whole land.[-a] 5 And do you expect great things for yourself? Don't expect them. For I am going to bring disaster upon all flesh—declares the LORD—but I will [b-]at least grant you your life[-b] in all the places where you may go.

46

1 The word of the LORD to the prophet Jeremiah concerning the nations.

2 Concerning Egypt, about the army of Pharaoh Neco, king of Egypt, which was at the river Euphrates near Carchemish, and which was defeated by King Nebuchadrezzar of Babylon, in the fourth year of King Jehoiakim son of Josiah of Judah.

3 Get ready buckler and shield,
  And move forward to battle!
4 Harness the horses;
  Mount, you horsemen!
  Fall in line, helmets on!
  Burnish the lances,
  Don your armor!
5 Why do I see them dismayed,
  Yielding ground?
  Their fighters are crushed,
  They flee in haste
  And do not turn back—
  Terror all around!
            —declares the LORD.

---

[a] See note at 24.9
[g-g] Lit. "spoken with your mouth and fulfilled by your hands"

[a-a] Meaning of Heb uncertain
[b-b] Cf. note at 21.9

6 ᵃ⁻The swift cannot get away,
  The warrior cannot escape.⁻ᵃ
  In the north, by the river Euphrates,
  They stagger and fall.

7 Who is this that rises like the Nile,
  Like streams whose waters surge?
8 It is Egypt that rises like the Nile,
  Like streams whose waters surge,
  That said, "I will rise,
  I will cover the earth,
  I will wipe out towns
  And those who dwell in them.
9 Advance, O horses,
  Dash madly, O chariots!
  Let the warriors go forth,
  Cush and Put, that grasp the shield,
  And the Ludim who grasp and draw the bow!"

10 But that day shall be for the Lord GOD of Hosts a day when He exacts retribution from His foes. The sword shall devour; it shall be sated and drunk with their blood. For the Lord GOD of Hosts is preparing a sacrifice in the northland, by the river Euphrates.

11 Go up to Gilead and get balm,
   Fair Maiden Egypt.
   In vain do you seek many remedies,
   There is no healing for you.
12 Nations have heard your shame;
   The earth resounds with your screams.
   For warrior stumbles against warrior;
   The two fall down together.

13 The word which the LORD spoke to the prophet Jeremiah about the coming of King Nebuchadrezzar of Babylon to attack the land of Egypt:

14 Declare in Egypt, proclaim in Migdol,
   Proclaim in Noph and Tahpanhes!
   Say: Take your posts and stand ready,
   For the sword has devoured all around you!
15 Why are your stalwarts swept away?
   They did not stand firm,
   For the LORD thrust them down;
16 He made many stumble,
   They fell over one another.

   They said:
   "Up! let us return to our people,
   To the land of our birth,
   Because of the deadlyᵇ sword."
17 There they called Pharaoh king of Egypt:
   "Braggart who let the hour go by."

18 As I live—declares the King,
   Whose name is LORD of Hosts—
   ᵇ⁻As surely as Tabor is among the mountains
   And Carmel is by the sea,
   So shall this come to pass.⁻ᵇ
19 Equip yourself for exile,
   Fair Egypt who dwell secure!
   For Noph shall become a waste,
   Desolate, without inhabitants.
20 Egypt is a handsome heifer—
   A gadflyᶜ from the north ᵈ⁻is coming, coming!⁻ᵈ
21 The mercenaries, too, in her midst
   Are like stall-fed calves;
   They too shall turn tail,
   Flee as one, and make no stand.
   Their day of disaster is upon them,
   The hour of their doom.
22 ᵇ⁻She shall rustle away like a snake⁻ᵇ
   As they come marching in force;
   They shall come against her with axes,
   Like hewers of wood.
23 They shall cut down her forest
                            —declares the LORD—
   Though it cannot be measured;
   For they are more numerous than locusts,
   And cannot be counted.
24 Fair Egypt shall be shamed,
   Handed over to the people of the north.

25 The LORD of Hosts, the God of Israel, has said: I will inflict punishment on Amonᵉ of No and on Pharaoh—on Egypt, her gods, and her kings—on

---

ᵃ⁻ᵃ Lit. "Let not the swift get away, / Let not the fighter escape"
ᵇ Meaning of Heb uncertain
ᶜ Or "butcher"; meaning of Heb uncertain
ᵈ⁻ᵈ Many mss. read "will come upon her"
ᵉ Tutelary deity of the city No (Thebes); cf. Nah. 3.8

Pharaoh and all who rely on him. ²⁶ I will deliver them to those who seek to kill them, to King Nebuchadrezzar of Babylon and his subjects. But afterward she shall be inhabited again as in former days, declares the LORD.

²⁷ But you,
Have no fear, My servant Jacob,
Be not dismayed, O Israel!
I will deliver you from far away,
Your folk from their land of captivity;
And Jacob again shall have calm
And quiet, with none to trouble him.
²⁸ But you, have no fear,
My servant Jacob
—declares the LORD—
For I am with you.
I will make an end of all the nations
Among which I have banished you,
But I will not make an end of you!
I will not leave you unpunished,
But I will chastise you in measure.

¹ The word of the LORD that came to the prophet Jeremiah concerning the Philistines, before Pharaoh conquered Gaza.

² Thus said the LORD:

See, waters are rising from the north,
They shall become a raging torrent,
They shall flood the land and its creatures,
The towns and their inhabitants.
Men shall cry out,
All the inhabitants of the land shall howl,
³ At the clatter of the stamping hoofs of his stallions,
At the noise of his chariots,
The rumbling of their wheels,
Fathers shall not look to their children
Out of ᵃ⁻sheer helplessness⁻ᵃ—
⁴ Because of the day that is coming
For ravaging all the Philistines,
For cutting off every last ally
Of Tyre and Sidon.
For the LORD will ravage the Philistines,
The remnant from the island of Caphtor.
⁵ Baldnessᵇ has come upon Gaza,
Ashkelon is destroyed.
O remnant of ᶜ⁻their valley,⁻ᶜ
How long will you ᵇ⁻gash yourself?⁻ᵇ

⁶ "O sword of the LORD,
When will you be quiet at last?
Withdraw into your sheath,
Rest and be still!"

⁷ How can itᵈ be quiet
When the LORD has given it orders
Against Ashkelon and the seacoast,
Given it assignment there?

48

¹ Concerning Moab.ᵃ

Thus said the LORD of Hosts, the God of Israel:
Alas, that Nebo should be ravaged,
Kiriathaim captured and shamed,
ᵇ⁻The stronghold⁻ᵇ shamed and dismayed!
² Moab's glory is no more;
In Heshbon they have plannedᶜ evil against her:
"Come, let us make an end of her as a nation!"
You too, O Madmen, shall be silenced;ᵈ
The sword is following you.
³ Hark! an outcry from Horonaim,
Destruction and utter ruin!

⁴ Moab is broken;
ᵉ⁻Her young ones cry aloud;⁻ᵉ

ᵃ⁻ᵃLit. "weakness of hands"
ᵇ⁻ᵇShaving the head and gashing the body were expressions of mourning
ᶜ⁻ᶜSeptuagint reads "the Anakim"; cf. Josh. 11.22
ᵈHeb "you"

ᵃA number of parallels to this chapter occur in Isa. 15–16
ᵇ⁻ᵇOr "Misgab"
ᶜHeb *hashebu*, play on Heshbon
ᵈHeb *tiddommi*, play on Madmen, the name of a town
ᵉ⁻ᵉEmendation yields "They cry aloud as far as Zoar"; cf. Isa. 15.5

JEREMIAH 48·5

5 They climb to Luhith
 Weeping continually;
 On the descent to Horonaim
 A distressing cry of anguish is heard:
6 Flee, save your lives!
 *ᶠ⁻*And be like Aroer in the desert.*⁻ᶠ*

7 Surely, because of your trust
 In your wealth and in your treasures,
 You too shall be captured.
 And Chemosh shall go forth to exile,
 Together with his priests and attendants.
8 The ravager shall come to every town;
 No town shall escape.
 The valley shall be devastated
 And the tableland laid waste
 —because the LORD has spoken.
9 Give *ᶠ⁻*wings to Moab,
 For she must go hence.*⁻ᶠ*
 Her towns shall become desolate,
 With no one living in them.

10 Cursed be he who is slack in doing the LORD's work! Cursed be he who withholds his sword from blood!

11 Moab has been secure from his youth on—
 He is settled on his lees
 And has not been poured from vessel to vessel—
 He has never gone into exile.
 Therefore his fine flavor has remained
 And his bouquet is unspoiled.

12 But days are coming—declares the LORD—when I will send men against him to tip him over; they shall empty his vessels and smash his jars. 13 And Moab shall be shamed because of Chemosh, as the House of Israel were shamed because of Bethel, on whom they relied.

14 How can you say: We are warriors,
 Valiant men for war?
15 Moab is ravaged,
 His towns have been entered,
 His choice young men
 Have gone down to the slaughter
 —declares the King whose name is
 LORD of Hosts.
16 The doom of Moab is coming close,
 His downfall is approaching swiftly.
17 Condole with him, all who live near him,
 All you who know him by name!
 Say: "Alas, the strong rod is broken,
 The lordly staff!"

18 Descend from glory
 And sit in thirst,*ᶠ*
 O inhabitant of Fair Dibon;
 For the ravager of Moab has entered your town,
 He has destroyed your fortresses.
19 Stand by the road and look out,
 O inhabitant of Aroer.
 Ask of him who is fleeing
 And of her who is escaping:
 Say, "What has happened?"
20 Moab is shamed and dismayed;
 Howl and cry aloud!
 Tell at the Arnon
 That Moab is ravaged!

21 Judgment has come upon the tableland—upon Holon, Jahzah, and Mephaath; 22 upon Dibon, Nebo, and Beth-diblathaim; 23 upon Kiriathaim, Beth-gamul, and Beth-meon; 24 upon Kerioth and Bozrah—upon all the towns of Moab, far and near.

25 The might of Moab has been cut down,
 His strength is broken
 —declares the LORD.
26 Get him drunk
 For he vaunted himself against the LORD.
 Moab shall wallow*ᶠ* in his vomit,
 And he too shall be a laughingstock.
27 Wasn't Israel a laughingstock to you?
 Was he ever caught among thieves,
 That you should *ᵍ⁻*shake your head*⁻ᵍ*
 Whenever you speak of him?

ᶠ⁻ᶠ Meaning of Heb uncertain
ᵍ⁻ᵍ I.e. in mockery

JEREMIAH 48·28

²⁸ Desert the cities
  And dwell in the crags,
  O inhabitants of Moab!
  Be like a dove that nests
  In the sides of a pit.

²⁹ We have heard of Moab's pride—
  Most haughty is he—
  Of his arrogance and pride,
  His haughtiness and self-exaltation.
³⁰ I know his insolence—declares the LORD—the wickedness that is in him,[h] the wickedness [i-he has-i] committed.
³¹ Therefore I will howl for Moab,
  I will cry out for all Moab,
  I[j] will moan for the men of Kir-heres.
³² With greater weeping than for Jazer
  I weep for you, O vine of Sibmah,
  Whose tendrils crossed the sea,
  Reached to the sea,[f] to Jazer.
  A ravager has come down
  Upon your fig and grape harvest.
³³ Rejoicing and gladness
  Are gone from the farmland,
  From the country of Moab;
  I have put an end to wine in the presses,
  No one treads [the grapes] with shouting—
  [f-The shout is a shout no more.-f]
³⁴ There is an outcry from Heshbon to Elealeh,
  They raise their voices as far as Jahaz,
  From Zoar to Horonaim and Eglath-shelishiah.
  The waters of Nimrim
  Shall also become desolation.
³⁵ And I shall make an end in Moab
              —declares the LORD—
  Of those who offer at a shrine
  And burn incense to their god.
³⁶ Like a flute my heart moans for Moab,
  Like a flute my heart moans for the men
              of Kir-heres.—
  [f-Therefore the gains they have made shall vanish.-f]—
³⁷ For every head is bald
  And every beard is shorn;
  On all hands there are gashes,
  And on the loins sackcloth.
³⁸ On all the roofs of Moab,
  And in its squares
  There is naught but lamentation;
  For I have broken Moab
  Like a vessel no one wants
              —declares the LORD.
³⁹ How he is dismayed! Wail!
  How Moab has turned his back in shame!
  Moab shall be a laughingstock
  And a shock to all those near him.

⁴⁰ For thus said the LORD:

  See, he soars like an eagle
  And spreads out his wings against Moab!
⁴¹ Kerioth shall be captured
  And the strongholds shall be seized.
  In that day, the heart of Moab's warriors
  Shall be like the heart of a woman in travail.
⁴² And Moab shall be destroyed as a people,
  For he vaunted himself against the LORD.
⁴³ [k-Terror, and pit, and trap-k]
  Upon you who dwell in Moab!
              —declares the LORD.
⁴⁴ He who flees from the terror
  Shall fall into the pit;
  And he who climbs out of the pit
  Shall be caught in the trap.
  For I will bring upon Moab
  The year of their doom
              —declares the LORD.

⁴⁵ In the shelter of Heshbon
  Fugitives halt exhausted;
  For fire went forth from Heshbon,
  Flame from the [l-midst of-l] Sihon,
  Consuming the brow of Moab,
  The pate of the people of Shaon.[m]
⁴⁶ Woe to you, O Moab!
  The people of Chemosh are undone,

---

f-f Meaning of Heb uncertain
h Cf. note at Isa. 16.6
i-i Heb "they have"
j Heb "He"
k-k See note at Isa. 24.17
l-l Emendation yields "house of"
m Or "tumult"

JEREMIAH 48·47

    For your sons are carried off into captivity,
      Your daughters into exile.
47 But I will restore the fortunes of Moab in the days to come—declares the LORD.

Thus far is the judgment on Moab.

49

¹ Concerning the Ammonites.

    Has Israel no sons,
    Has he no heir?
    Then why has Milcom*ᵃ* dispossessed Gad,
    And why have his people settled in Gad's*ᵇ* towns?
² Assuredly, days are coming
                  —declares the LORD—
    When I will sound the alarm of war
    Against Rabbah of the Ammonites;
    It shall become a desolate mound,
    And its villages shall be set on fire.
    And Israel shall dispossess
    Those who dispossessed him
                  —said the LORD.
³ Howl, O Heshbon, for Ai is ravaged!
    Cry out, O daughters of Rabbah!
    Gird on sackcloth, lament,
    ᶜ⁻And run to and fro in the sheepfolds.⁻*ᶜ*
    For Milcom shall go into exile,
    Together with his priests and attendants.

⁴ *ᵈ*⁻Why do you glory in strength,
    Your strength is drained,⁻*ᵈ*
    O rebellious daughter,
    You who relied on your treasures,
    [Who said:] Who dare attack me?
⁵ I am bringing terror upon you
              —declares the Lord GOD of Hosts—
    From all those around you.
    Every one of you shall be driven *ᵉ*⁻in every direction,⁻*ᵉ*
    And none shall gather in the fugitives.
⁶ But afterwards I will restore the fortunes of the Ammonites—declares the LORD.

⁷ Concerning Edom.

    Thus said the LORD of Hosts:
    Is there no more wisdom in Teman?
    Has counsel vanished from the prudent?
    Has their wisdom gone stale?
⁸ Flee, turn away, sit down low,
    O inhabitants of Dedan,
    For I am bringing Esau's doom upon him,
    The time when I deal with him.
⁹ *ᶠ*⁻If vintagers were to come upon you,
    Would they leave no gleanings?
    Even thieves in the night
    Would destroy only for their needs!
¹⁰ But it is I have bared Esau,
    Have exposed his place of concealment;
    He cannot hide.
    His offspring is ravaged,
    His kin and his neighbors—
    ᵍ⁻He is no more.⁻*ᵍ*
¹¹ "Leave your orphans with me,
    I will rear them;
    Let your widows rely on me!"
¹² For thus said the LORD: If they who rightly should not drink of the cup must drink it, are you the one to go unpunished? You shall not go unpunished: you will have to drink! ¹³ For by Myself I swear—declares the LORD—Bozrah shall become a desolation, a mockery, a ruin, and a curse;*ʰ* and all its towns shall be ruins for all time.

¹⁴ I have received tidings from the LORD,
    And an envoy is sent out among the nations:
    Assemble, and move against her,
    And rise up for war!
¹⁵ For I will make you least among nations,
    Most despised among men.
¹⁶ *ᵉ*⁻Your horrible nature,⁻*ᵉ*
    Your arrogant heart has seduced you,

---

*ᵃ*The name of the Ammonite deity; vocalized Malcam here and in v. 3
*ᵇ*Heb "his"
*ᶜ⁻ᶜ*Meaning of Heb uncertain
*ᵈ⁻ᵈ*Meaning of Heb uncertain; for "strength" cf. Akkadian *emuqu*
*ᵉ⁻ᵉ*Lit. "each man straight ahead"
*ᶠ*Obadiah 1.5 reads: "If thieves were to come to you, / Marauders by night, / They would steal no more than they needed. / If vintagers came to you, / They would surely leave some gleanings"
*ᵍ⁻ᵍ*Some Septuagint mss. read "And there is none to say"
*ʰ*Cf. note at 24.9 and 42.18

JEREMIAH 49.17

You who dwell in clefts of the rock,
Who occupy the height of the hill!
Should you nest as high as the eagle,
From there I will pull you down
—declares the LORD.

17 And Edom shall be a cause of appallment; whoever passes by will be appalled and will hiss[i] at all its wounds. 18 It shall be like the overthrow of Sodom and Gomorrah and their neighbors—said the LORD: no man shall live there, no human shall sojourn there. 19 It shall be as when a lion comes up out of the jungle of the Jordan against a secure pasture: in a moment [j-]I can harry him out of it and appoint over it anyone I choose.[-j] Then who is like Me? Who can summon Me? Who is the shepherd that can stand up against Me? 20 Hear, then, the plan which the LORD has devised against Edom, and what He has purposed against the inhabitants of Teman:

Surely the shepherd boys
Shall drag them away;
Surely the pasture shall be
Aghast because of them.
21 At the sound of their downfall
The earth shall shake;
The sound of screaming
Shall be heard at the Sea of Reeds.
22 See, like an eagle he flies up,
He soars and spreads his wings against Bozrah;
And the heart of Edom's warriors in that day
Shall be like the heart of a woman in travail.

23 Concerning Damascus.

Hamath and Arpad are shamed,
For they have heard bad news.
They shake with anxiety,
Like[k] the sea which cannot rest.
24 Damascus has grown weak,
She has turned around to flee;
Trembling has seized her,
Pain and anguish have taken hold of her,
Like a woman in childbirth.
25 [l-]How has the glorious city not been deserted,[-l]
The citadel of my joy!
26 Assuredly, her young men shall lie fallen in
her squares.
And all her warriors shall be stilled in that day
—declares the LORD of Hosts.
27 I will set fire to the wall of Damascus,
And it shall consume the fortresses of Ben-hadad.

28 Concerning Kedar and the kingdoms of Hazor, which King Nebuchadrezzar of Babylon conquered.

Thus said the LORD:

Arise, march against Kedar,
And ravage the Kedemites!
29 They will take away their tents and their flocks,
Their tent cloths and all their gear;
They shall carry off their camels,
And shall proclaim against them:
Terror all around!
30 Flee, wander far,
Sit down low, O inhabitants of Hazor
—declares the LORD.
For King Nebuchadrezzar of Babylon
Has devised a plan against you
And formed a purpose against you:
31 Rise up, attack a tranquil nation
That dwells secure
—declares the LORD—
That has no barred gates,
That dwells alone.
32 Their camels shall become booty,
And their abundant flocks a spoil;
And I will scatter to every quarter
Those who have their hair clipped;
And from every direction I will bring
Disaster upon them
—declares the LORD.
33 Hazor shall become a lair of jackals,
A desolation for all time.
No man shall live there,
No human shall sojourn there.

[i] Cf. note at 18.16
[j-j] Emendation yields "he can harry them [i.e. the sheep] out of it; and what champion could one place in charge of them?"
[k] So a few mss. Most mss. and editions read "In"
[l-l] Emendation yields "How has the glorious city been deserted"; so Vulgate

JEREMIAH 49.34

³⁴ The word of the LORD that came to the prophet Jeremiah concerning Elam, at the beginning of the reign of King Zedekiah of Judah:

³⁵ Thus said the LORD of Hosts: I am going to break the bow of Elam, the mainstay of their strength. ³⁶ And I shall bring four winds against Elam from the four quarters of heaven, and scatter them to all those winds. There shall not be a nation to which the fugitives from Elam do not come. ³⁷ And I will put Elam to dismay before their enemies, before those who seek their lives; and I will bring upon them disaster, My flaming wrath—declares the LORD. And I will dispatch the sword after them until I have consumed them.

³⁸ And I will set My throne in Elam,
And wipe out from there king and officials
—declares the LORD.

³⁹ But in the days to come I will restore the fortunes of Elam—declares the LORD.

50

¹ The word which the LORD spoke concerning Babylon, the land of the Chaldeans, through the prophet Jeremiah;

² Declare among the nations, and proclaim;
Raise a standard, proclaim;
Hide nothing! Say:
Babylon is captured,
Bel is shamed,
Merodach is dismayed.
Her idols are shamed,
Her fetishes dismayed.
³ For a nation from the north has attacked her,
It will make her land a desolation.
No one shall dwell in it,
Both man and beast shall wander away.

⁴ In those days and at that time—declares the LORD—the people of Israel together with the people of Judah shall come, and they shall weep as they go to seek the LORD their God. ⁵ They shall inquire for Zion; in that direction their faces shall turn; ᵃ⁻they shall come⁻ᵃ and attach themselves to the LORD by a covenant for all time, which shall never be forgotten. ⁶ My people were lost sheep: their shepherds led them astray, they drove them out to the mountains, they roamed from mount to hill, they forgot their own resting place. ⁷ All who encountered them devoured them; and their foes said, "We shall not be held guilty, because they have sinned against the LORD, the true Pasture, the Hope of their fathers—the LORD."

⁸ Flee from Babylon,
Leave the land of the Chaldeans,
And be like he-goats that lead the flock!
⁹ For see, I am rousing and leading
An assemblage of great nations against Babylon
From the lands of the north.
They shall draw up their lines against her,
There she shall be captured.
Their arrows are like those of ᵇ⁻a deadly warrior⁻ᵇ
Who does not turn back without hitting the mark.
¹⁰ Chaldea shall be despoiled,
All her spoilers shall be sated
—declares the LORD.
¹¹ For you rejoiced, you exulted,
You who plundered My possession;
You stamped like a heifer treading grain,
You neighed like steeds.
¹² So your mother will be utterly shamed,
She who bore you will be disgraced.
Behold the end of the nations—
Wilderness, desert, and steppe!
¹³ Because of the LORD's wrath she shall not
be inhabited;
She shall be utterly desolate.
Whoever passes by will be appalled
And will hissᶜ at all her wounds.

¹⁴ Range yourselves round about Babylon,
All you who draw the bow;
Shoot at her, don't spare arrows,

ᵃ⁻ᵃHeb "come ye"
ᵇ⁻ᵇSo many mss., editions, and versions; other mss. and editions read "a warrior who bereaves"
ᶜCf. note at 18.16

JEREMIAH 50·15

For she has sinned against the LORD.
15 Raise a shout against her all about!
   *ᵈ⁻*She has surrendered;⁻ᵈ
   Her bastions have fallen,
   Her walls are thrown down—
   This is the LORD's vengeance.
   Take vengeance on her,
   Do to her as she has done!
16 Make an end in Babylon of sowers,
   And of wielders of the sickle at harvest time.
   Because of the deadlyᵉ sword,
   Each man shall turn back to his people,
   They shall flee every one to his land.

17 Israel are scattered sheep, harried by lions. First the king of Assyria devoured them, and in the end King Nebuchadrezzar of Babylon crunched their bones. 18 Assuredly, thus said the LORD of Hosts, the God of Israel, I will deal with the king of Babylon and his land as I dealt with the king of Assyria. 19 And I will lead Israel back to his pasture, and he shall graze in Carmel and Bashan, and eat his fill in the hill country of Ephraim and in Gilead.
20 In those days and at that time
                              —declares the LORD—
   The iniquity of Israel shall be sought,
   And there shall be none;
   The sins of Judah,
   And none shall be found;
   For I will pardon those I allow to survive.

21 Advance against the land of Merathaim,
   And against the inhabitants of Pekod;
   Ruin and destroy after them to the last
                              —declares the LORD—
   Do just as I have commanded you.
22 Hark! War in the land
   And vast destruction!
23 How the hammer of the whole earth
   Has been hacked and shattered!
   How Babylon has become
   An appallment among the nations!
24 I set a snare for you, O Babylon,
   And you were trapped unawares;
   You were found and caught,
   Because you challenged the LORD.
25 The LORD has opened His armory
   And brought out the weapons of His wrath;
   For that is the task
   Of my Lord GOD of Hosts
   In the land of the Chaldeans.
26 Come against her *ᵉ⁻*from every quarter;⁻ᵉ
   Break open her granaries,
   *ᵉ⁻*Pile her up like heaps of grain,⁻ᵉ
   And destroy her, let her have no remnant!
27 *ᶠ⁻*Destroy all⁻ᶠ her bulls,
   Let them go down to slaughter.
   Alas for them, their day is come,
   The hour of their doom!
28 Hark! fugitives are escaping
   From the land of Babylon,
   To tell in Zion of the vengeance of the LORD our God,
   Vengeance for His Temple.

29 Summon archers against Babylon,
   All who draw the bow!
   Encamp against her round about,
   Let none of her people escape.
   Pay her back for her actions,
   Do to her just what she has done;
   For she has acted insolently against the LORD,
   The Holy One of Israel.
30 Assuredly, her young men shall fall in her squares,
   And all her warriors shall perish in that day
                              —declares the LORD.
31 See, I am against you, O Insolence
                              —declares the Lord GOD of Hosts—
   For your day is come, the time when I doom you:
32 Insolence shall stumble and fall,
   With none to raise her up.
   I will set her cities on fire,
   And it shall consume everything around her.

33 Thus said the LORD of Hosts:
   The people of Israel are oppressed,
   And so too the people of Judah;
   All their captors held them,

ᵈ⁻ᵈ Lit. "She has given her hand"; meaning of Heb uncertain
ᵉ Meaning of Heb uncertain
ᶠ⁻ᶠ Emendation yields "A sword against"; cf. vv. 35 ff.

JEREMIAH 50.34

They refused to let them go.
³⁴ Their Redeemer is mighty,
His name is LORD of Hosts.
He will champion their cause—
So as to give rest to the earth,
And unrest to the inhabitants of Babylon.

³⁵ A sword against the Chaldeans
                  —declares the LORD—
And against the inhabitants of Babylon,
Against its officials and its wise men!
³⁶ A sword against the diviners, that they be made
    fools of!
A sword against the warriors, that they be dismayed!
³⁷ A sword against its horses and chariots,
And against all the motley crowd in its midst,
That they become like women!
A sword against its treasuries, that they be pillaged!
³⁸ A drought[g] against its waters, that they be dried up!
For it is a land of idols;
They are besotted by their [e-]dread images.[-e]
³⁹ Assuredly,
[e-]Beasts and jackals[-e] shall dwell [there],
And ostriches shall dwell there;
It shall never be settled again,
Nor inhabited throughout the ages.
⁴⁰ It shall be as when God overthrew Sodom and Gomorrah and their neighbors—declares the LORD; no man shall live there, no human shall sojourn there.

⁴¹ Lo, a people comes from the northland;
A great nation and many kings are roused
From the remotest parts of the earth.
⁴² They grasp the bow and javelin,
They are cruel, they show no mercy;
The sound of them is like the roaring sea.
They ride upon horses,
Accoutered like a man for battle,
Against you, O Fair Babylon!
⁴³ The king of Babylon has heard the report of them,
And his hands are weakened;
Anguish seizes him,
Pangs like a woman in childbirth.

⁴⁴ It shall be as when a lion comes out of the jungle of the Jordan against a secure pasture: in a moment [h-]I can harry them out of it and appoint over it anyone I choose.[-h] Then who is like Me? Who can summon Me? Who is the shepherd that can stand against Me? ⁴⁵ Hear, then, the plan which the LORD has devised against Babylon, and has purposed against the land of Chaldea:
Surely the shepherd boys shall drag them away,
Surely the pasture shall be
Aghast because of them.
⁴⁶ At the sound of Babylon's capture
The earth quakes,
And an outcry is heard among the nations.

51

¹ Thus said the LORD:

See, I am rousing a destructive wind
Against Babylon and the inhabitants of Leb-kamai.[a]
² I will send strangers[b] against Babylon, and they
                          shall winnow her.
And they shall strip her land bare;
They shall beset her on all sides
On the day of disaster.
³ Let[c] the archer draw his bow,
And let him stand ready in his coat of mail!
Show no pity to her young men,
Wipe out all her host!
⁴ Let them fall slain in the land of Chaldea,
Pierced through in her streets.

⁵ For Israel and Judah were not bereft[d]
Of their God the LORD of Hosts,
But their land was filled with guilt
Before the Holy One of Israel.

⁶ Flee from the midst of Babylon
And save your lives, each of you!

[e-e] Meaning of Heb uncertain
[g] *Horeb*, play on *hereb*, "sword" in preceding verses
[h-h] See note at 49.19

[a] A cipher for *Kasdim*, "Chaldea"
[b] Change of vocalization yields "winnowers"
[c] Some Heb mss. and ancient versions read "Let not" here and in next line
[d] Lit. "widowed"

JEREMIAH 51·7

Do not perish for her iniquity;
For this is a time of vengeance for the LORD,
He will deal retribution to her.

7 Babylon was a golden cup in the LORD's hand,
It made the whole earth drunk;
The nations drank of her wine—
That is why the nations are mad.
8 Suddenly Babylon has fallen and is shattered;
Howl over her!
Get balm for her wounds:
Perhaps she can be healed.
9 We tried to cure Babylon
But she was incurable.
Let us leave her and go,
Each to his own land;
For her punishment reaches to heaven,
It is as high as the sky.
10 The LORD has proclaimed our vindication;
Come, let us recount in Zion
The deeds of the LORD our God.

11 Polish the arrows,
Fill the quivers!ᵉ
The LORD has roused the spirit of the kings of Media,
For His plan against Babylon is to destroy her.
This is the vengeance of the LORD,
Vengeance for His Temple.

12 Raise a standard against the walls of Babylon!
Set up a blockade, station watchmen,
Prepare those in ambush;
For the LORD has both planned and performed
What He decreed against the inhabitants of Babylon.

13 O you who dwell by great waters,
With vast storehouses,
Your time is come, ᵉ⁻the hour of your end.⁻ᵉ
14 The LORD of Hosts has sworn by Himself:
I will fill you with men like a locust swarm,
They will raise a shout against you.

15 He made the earth by His might,
Established the world by His wisdom,
And by His understanding stretched out the skies.
16 ᶠ⁻When He makes His voice heard,⁻ᶠ
There is a rumbling of waters in the skies;
He makes vapors rise from the end of the earth,
He makes lightning for the rain,
And brings forth wind from His treasuries.
17 Every man is proved dull, without knowledge;
Every goldsmith is put to shame because of the idol,
For his molten image is a deceit—
There is no breath in them.
18 They are delusion, a work of mockery;
In the hour of their doom, they shall perish.
19 Not like these is the Portion of Jacob,
For it is He who formed all things;
And [Israel is] His very own tribe.
LORD of Hosts is His name.

20 You are My war club, [My] weapons of battle;
With you I clubbed nations,
With you I destroyed kingdoms;
21 With you I clubbed horse and rider,
With you I clubbed chariot and driver,
22 With you I clubbed man and woman,
With you I clubbed graybeard and boy,
With you I clubbed youth and maiden;
23 With you I clubbed shepherd and flock,
With you I clubbed plowman and team,
With you I clubbed governors and prefects.

24 But I will requite Babylon and all the inhabitants
of Chaldea
For all the wicked things they did to Zion before
your eyes
—declares the LORD.
25 See, I will deal with you, O mountain of the destroyer
—declares the LORD—
Destroyer of the whole earth!
I will stretch out My hand against you
And roll you down from the crags,
And make you a burnt-out mountain.
26 They shall never take from you
A cornerstone or foundation stone;
You shall be a desolation for all time
—declares the LORD.
27 Raise a standard on earth,
Sound a horn among the nations,
Appoint nations against her,

ᵉ⁻ᵉ Meaning of Heb uncertain   ᶠ⁻ᶠ Lit. "At the sound of his making"

JEREMIAH 51·28

Assemble kingdoms against her—
Ararat, Minni, and Ashkenaz—
Designate a marshal against her,
Bring up horses like swarming[e] locusts!
[28] Appoint nations for war against her—
The kings of Media,
Her governors and all her prefects,
And all the lands they rule!

[29] Then the earth quakes and writhes,
For the LORD's purpose is fulfilled against Babylon,
To make the land of Babylon
A waste without inhabitant.
[30] The warriors of Babylon stop fighting,
They sit in the strongholds,
Their might is dried up,
They become women.
Her dwellings are set afire,
Her bars are broken.
[31] Runner dashes to meet runner,
Messenger to meet messenger,
To report to the king of Babylon
That his city is captured, from end to end.
[32] The fords are captured,
And the swamp thickets[e] are consumed in fire;
And the fighting men are in panic.

[33] For thus said the LORD of Hosts, the God of Israel:
Fair Babylon is like a threshing floor
Ready to be trodden;
In a little while her harvest time will come.

[34] "Nebuchadrezzar king of Babylon
Devoured me and discomfited me;
He swallowed me like a dragon,
He filled his belly with my dainties,
And set me down like an empty dish;
Then he [e-]rinsed me out.[-e]
[35] Let the violence done me and my kindred
Be upon Babylon,"
Says the inhabitant of Zion;
"And let my blood be upon the inhabitants
                                                of Chaldea,"
Says Jerusalem.

[36] Assuredly, thus said the LORD:
I am going to uphold your cause
And take vengeance for you;
I will dry up her sea
And make her fountain run dry.
[37] Babylon shall become rubble,
A den for jackals,
An object of horror and hissing,[g]
Without inhabitant.
[38] Like lions, they roar together,
They growl like lion cubs.
[39] [h-]When they are heated, I will set out their drink
And get them drunk, that they may become hilarious[-h]
And then sleep an endless sleep,
Never to awake
                                                —declares the LORD.
[40] I will bring them down like lambs for slaughter,
Like rams and he-goats.
[41] How has Sheshach[i] been captured,
The praise of the whole earth been taken!
How has Babylon become
A horror to the nations!
[42] The sea has risen over Babylon,
She is covered by its roaring waves.
[43] Her towns are a desolation,
A land of desert and steppe,
A land no man lives in
And no human passes through.
[44] And I will deal with Bel in Babylon,
And make him disgorge what he has swallowed,
And nations shall no more gaze on him with joy.
Even the wall of Babylon shall fall.

[45] Go out from there, O My people,
Save your lives, each of you,
From the furious anger of the LORD.
[46] Do not be downhearted or afraid
At the rumors heard in the land:
A rumor will come one year,
And another rumor the next year
Of violence in the land,
And of ruler against ruler.

[e-e] Meaning of Heb uncertain
[g] See note at 18.16
[h-h] Emendation yields "With poison [so Syriac] will I set out their drink /
And get them drunk till they fall unconscious" (so ancient versions)
[i] See note at 25.26

JEREMIAH 51·47

47 Assuredly, days are coming,
  When I will deal with Babylon's images;
  Her whole land shall be shamed,
  And all her slain shall fall in her midst.
48 Heavens and earth and all that is in them
  Shall shout over Babylon;
  For the ravagers shall come upon her from the north
    —declares the LORD.
49 Yes, Babylon is to fall
  [For] the slain of Israel,
  As the slain of all the earth
  Have fallen through Babylon.

50 You fugitives from the sword,
  Go, don't delay!
  Remember the LORD from afar,
  And call Jerusalem to mind.
51 "We were shamed, we heard taunts;
  Humiliation covered our faces,
  When aliens entered
  The sacred areas of the LORD's House."
52 Assuredly, days are coming
    —declares the LORD—
  When I will deal with her images,
  And throughout her land the dying shall groan.
53 Though Babylon should climb to the skies,
  Though she fortify her strongholds up to heaven,
  The ravagers would come against her from Me
    —declares the LORD.

54 Hark! an outcry from Babylon,
  Great destruction from the land of the Chaldeans.
55 For the LORD is ravaging Babylon;
  He will put an end to her great din,
  Whose roar is like waves of mighty waters,
  Whose tumultuous noise resounds.
56 For a ravager is coming upon Babylon,
  Her warriors shall be captured, their bows shall
    be snapped.
  For the LORD is a God of requital,
  He deals retribution.
57 I will make her officials and wise men drunk,
  Her governors and prefects and warriors;
  And they shall sleep an endless sleep,
  Never to awaken
    —declares the King whose name is
      LORD of Hosts.
58 Thus said the LORD of Hosts:
  Babylon's broad wall shall be knocked down,
  And her high gates set afire.
  Peoples shall labor for naught,
  And nations have wearied themselves for fire.

59 The instructions which the prophet Jeremiah gave to Seraiah son of Neriah son of Mahseiah, when the latter went with[j] Zedekiah, king of Judah, to Babylonia, in the fourth year of [Zedekiah's] reign. Seraiah was quartermaster.[e] 60 Jeremiah wrote down in one scroll all the disaster that would come upon Babylon, all these things which are written concerning Babylon. 61 And Jeremiah said to Seraiah, "When you get to Babylon, see that you read out all these words. 62 And say, 'O LORD, You Yourself have declared concerning this place that it shall be cut off, without inhabitant, man or beast; that it shall be a desolation for all time.' 63 And when you finish reading this scroll, tie a stone to it and hurl it into the Euphrates. 64 And say, 'Thus shall Babylon sink and never rise again, because of the disaster which I will bring upon it. And [nations] shall have wearied themselves [for fire].' "[k]

Thus far the words of Jeremiah.

52

1[a] Zedekiah was twenty-one years old when he became king, and he reigned in Jerusalem for eleven years. His mother's name was Hamutal, daughter of Jeremiah of Libnah. 2 He did what was displeasing to the LORD, just as Jehoiakim had done. 3 Indeed, Jerusalem and Judah [b-]were a cause of anger for the LORD, so that[-b] He cast them out of His presence.

---
[e] Meaning of Heb uncertain
[j] Emendation yields "at the instance of"
[k] Cf. v. 58, last line

[a] For this chapter cf. chapter 39 above and II Kings 25
[b-b] Meaning of Heb uncertain

JEREMIAH 52.4

Zedekiah rebelled against the king of Babylon. ⁴ And in the ninth year of his[c] reign, on the tenth day of the tenth month, King Nebuchadrezzar came up against Jerusalem with his whole army. They besieged it and built towers against it all around. ⁵ The city continued in a state of siege until the eleventh year of King Zedekiah. ⁶ By the ninth day of the fourth month, the famine had become acute in the city; there was no food left for the common people.

⁷ Then [the wall of] the city was breached. All the soldiers fled; they left the city by night through the gate between the double walls, which is near the king's garden—the Chaldeans were all around the city—and they set out for the Arabah.[d] ⁸ But the Chaldean troops pursued the king, and they overtook Zedekiah in the steppes of Jericho, as his entire force left him and scattered. ⁹ They captured the king and brought him before the king of Babylon at Riblah, in the region of Hamath; and he put him on trial. ¹⁰ The king of Babylon had Zedekiah's sons slaughtered before his eyes; he also had all the officials of Judah slaughtered at Riblah. ¹¹ Then the eyes of Zedekiah were put out, and he was chained in bronze fetters. The king of Babylon brought him to Babylon and put him in prison. [where he remained] to the day of his death.

¹² On the tenth day of the fifth month—that was the nineteenth year of King Nebuchadrezzar, the king of Babylon—Nebuzaradan, the chief of the guards, came [e-]to represent[-e] the king of Babylon in Jerusalem. ¹³ He burned the House of the LORD, the king's palace, and all the houses of Jerusalem; he burned down the house of [b-]every notable person.[-b] ¹⁴ The entire Chaldean force that was with the chief of the guards tore down all the walls of Jerusalem on every side. ¹⁵ The remnant of the people left in the city, the defectors who had gone over to the king of Babylon, and what remained of the craftsmen[f] were taken into exile by Nebuzaradan, the chief of the guards. But some of the poorest elements of the population— ¹⁶ some of the poorest in the land—were left by Nebuzaradan, the chief of the guards, to be vinedressers and field hands.

¹⁷ The Chaldeans broke up the bronze columns of the House of the LORD, the stands, and the bronze tank that was in the House of the LORD; and they carried all the bronze away to Babylon. ¹⁸ They also took the pails, the scrapers, the snuffers, the sprinkling bowls, the ladles, and the other bronze vessels used in the service. ¹⁹ The chief of the guards took whatever was of gold and whatever was of silver: basins, fire pans, sprinkling bowls, pails, lampstands, ladles, and jars. ²⁰ The two columns, the one tank and the twelve bronze oxen which supported it, and the stands, which King Solomon had provided for the House of the LORD— all these objects contained bronze beyond weighing. ²¹ As for the columns, each was eighteen cubits high and twelve cubits in circumference; it was hollow, and [the metal] was four fingers thick. ²² It had a bronze capital above it; the height of each capital was five cubits, and there was a meshwork [decorated] with pomegranates about the capital, all made of bronze; and so for the second column, also with pomegranates. ²³ There were ninety-six pomegranates [b-]facing outward;[-b] all the pomegranates around the meshwork amounted to one hundred.

²⁴ The chief of the guards took Seraiah the chief priest and Zephaniah the deputy priest, and the three guardians of the threshold. ²⁵ From the city he took a eunuch who was in command of the soldiers; seven royal privy councilors, who were found in the city; the scribe of the army commander, who was in charge of mustering the people of the land; and sixty of the common people who were inside the city. ²⁶ Nebuzaradan, the chief of the guards, took them and brought them to the king of Babylon at Riblah. ²⁷ The king of Babylon had them struck down and put to death at Riblah, in the region of Hamath.

[b-b]Meaning of Heb uncertain
[c]I.e. Zedekiah's
[d]See note at 39.4
[e-e]Lit. "he stood before"
[f]Apparently after the deportation of II Kings 24.14; meaning of Heb uncertain

JEREMIAH 52·28

Thus Judah was exiled from its land. ²⁸ This is the number of those whom Nebuchadrezzar exiled in the seventh year: 3,023 Judeans. ²⁹ In the eighteenth year of Nebuchadrezzar, 832 persons [were exiled] from Jerusalem. ³⁰ And in the twenty-third year of Nebuchadrezzar, Nebuzaradan, the chief of the guards, exiled 745 Judeans. The total amounted to 4,600 persons.

³¹ In the thirty-seventh year after King Jehoiachin of Judah was exiled, on the twenty-fifth day of the twelfth month, King Evil-merodach of Babylon, in the year he became king, *ᵍ⁻*took note of*⁻ᵍ* King Jehoiachin of Judah and released him from prison. ³² He spoke kindly to him, and gave him a throne above those of other kings who were with him in Babylon. ³³ So he removed his prison garments and ate regularly in his presence the rest of his life. ³⁴ A regular allotment of food was given him by order of the king of Babylon, on each day what was proper to it, to the day of his death—all the days of his life.

*ᵍ⁻ᵍ*Lit. "raised the head of"

CATHOLIC THEOLOGICAL UNION
OVERSIZE.BS1523.J481973   C001
[YIRMEYAH (ROMANIZED FORM)] [1ST ED.]

3 0311 00079 4490

51952

Oversize
BS   Bible. O.T. Jeremiah. Eng.
1523   Jewish Publication Society.
.J48   or 1973.
1973   THE BOOK OF JREMIAH :
TITLE   A NEW TRANSLATION.